FIGHTING
FIT
1914

Edited by Adam Culling

First published 2014

Amberley Publishing
The Hill, Stroud
Gloucestershire, GL5 4EP

www.amberleybooks.com

British Library Cataloguing in Publication Data.
A catalogue record for this book is available from the British Library.

ISBN 978-1-4456-3759-4 (paperback)
ISBN 978-1-4456-3773-0 (ebook)

Typesetting and Origination by Amberley Publishing.
Printed in the UK.

Contents

I

Fighting Fit! Physical Training in the British Army, 1860-1914

In today's society, the idea of explaining the need for physical conditioning in the British Army seems somewhat unnecessary. Visualising the British solider conjures up an image of physical robustness. But why is this so? Representations of the British solider in period dramas and action films would suggest that this has always been the case, but this is simply not true. At the outbreak of the First World War, physical training in the British Army, although mandated and carried out under the supervision of the Army Gymnastic Staff (AGS), was still in its infancy. No less than sixty-five years earlier this formally mandated, standardised and scientific military physical training did not exist.

That is not to say that no physical training or exercise took place in the British Army prior to the formation of the AGS in 1860. It would be equally absurd to suggest that soldiers were not fed before the formation of the Army Catering Corps (ACC) in 1942. Prior to the formation of the ACC responsibility for feeding the Army fell to other corps. Similarly, although there were no staff responsible for physical training in the Army prior to 1860, training did take place, although its form and duration varied among regiments and between officers and other ranks.

Participating in sports and games was common among British Army officers during the early nineteenth century and throughout Queen Victoria's reign. Field sports such as hunting, shooting and horse racing formed part of the original programme of military training; as many British officers during the nineteenth century came from the rural upper classes, it seemed appropriate that their values and pastimes would follow them into life in the Army. Officers would spend a tremendous amount of time occupied by sport, often more than they spent on their military duties. It was not uncommon for an officer to take more than six months of leave from military commitments during a year, and military commanders would authorise extended periods of leave for hunts and other sporting activities.[1]. Sports would even continue during wartime; for example, Major-General R. S. S. Baden-Powell, in his book *Sport in War*, describes suspending military operations while serving in Africa so he could hunt lions.[2]

Members of the rural upper class, from which many a British officer originated, would mostly have been educated in British public schools, and as such were subjected to the 'cult of games' that stemmed from these institutions. Sport and this culture of athleticism were, and still are, key to both school and military life and it is therefore of little surprise that the 'cult of games' carried over into their lives as officers. Officers believed that the value of sport and games helped to build character and physical prowess, both of which were considered crucial attributes of a successful combat leader and therefore formed part of a British officer's professional development.[3]

Mismanagement and poor leadership within the British Army during the Crimean War motivated political reformers to improve the Army. The reforms included eliminating flogging as a punishment, addressing the recruiting problems, restructuring the administrative and command hierarchy, abolishing the system of purchasing commissions, and finally – and most applicable in the understanding the origins of physical training – improving the health, living conditions and morale of the British soldier. Reports regarding soldiers' deaths from disease and infection in Crimea, and similarly poor conditions of garrisons in peacetime, led to one of many reform efforts. One successful reform was to provide troops with a healthy alternative to drinking and promiscuity, thus making the soldiers stronger and less susceptible to disease. As the voices of political and social reform grew louder, Palmerston's government reacted by creating the Army Sanitary Commission. Its members, selected by Florence Nightingale, were tasked with investigating and recommending solutions to the medical and sanitary problems that were brought to light during the Crimean War.[4]

The efforts of the Army Sanitary Commission focused on the restructuring and professionalisation of the Army Medical Department; the start of new construction programs including building hygienic barracks; improving the diet, cooking techniques, and messing arrangements of soldiers; and a recommendation for physical training to be adopted by the Army to assist in improving the general health and physical conditions of the soldiers.[5]

The latter of these efforts was the most significant for the development of the culture of physical training in the British Army. This particular recommendation was based upon several findings by the commission, such as recognising the benefits of physical training in improving a soldier's physical strength, and therefore increasing their resistance to disease. The recommendation was also based upon the apparent lower physical standards found among new recruits during the mid- and later nineteenth century. The strapping farmhands that served in the ranks of the British Army during the early nineteenth century had been replaced by smaller and less physically able recruits from the urban lower classes. This situation was exacerbated by the pressing need for soldiers during the Crimean War, which forced the Army to reduce the physical standards required for new recruits. Military commanders found that these new soldiers were incapable of performing the strenuous tasks required of them and were more likely to succumb to sickness and disease.[6] For many of these new recruits, physical training did not extend past marching and drill.

Physical conditioning was not the only reason for the introduction of mandated physical training in the British Army. A moral reform was also a driving force for change. The low moral standards of the British Army have been adequately documented; society held enlisted men in very low regard, often perceiving them as no more than immoral, alcoholic, promiscuous criminals. As the social reform of Britain's working class gathered pace in the mid- and late nineteenth century, attention soon turned to the Army.

Various solutions were offered to the moral problems found in the Army, including the introduction of 'Soldiers Homes', which provided an alternative to drinking alcohol or visiting brothels.[7] It was hoped that the establishment of temperance societies, regimental schools and regimental reading rooms would help lessen the immoral activities of the British soldier. These measures were not solely introduced to appease moral reformers – venereal disease (VD) was a serious problem for military commanders as it had a direct effect on the readiness of the Army. VD accounted for the loss of the equivalent to two full battalions a year and its treatment posed a significant financial burden. Regimental brothels for 'clean' women were introduced in garrison towns and so were financial penalties for soldiers who contracted VD.[8] All of these measures had limited success.

The most effective and lasting solution to the Army's moral issues was the introduction of mandatory gymnastics and voluntary regimental sports for all ranks. It was hoped that the Army would see improvements in the soldiers' general health and physical robustness, morale and moral character. If sports and games improved the leadership, fighting spirit, camaraderie and character of officers, military commanders anticipated that it would have the same effect on those in the ranks.[9]

The call for a formal programme of physical training in the British Army in the 1850s gained momentum. In 1859, Colonel F. W. Hamilton and Dr T. G. Logan, Inspector General to Hospitals, were sent by the War Office to France and Prussia to compile reports on the effectiveness of the gymnastic training systems of these armies. Both the French and Prussian armies introduced their formal military gymnastics training programmes in 1842, with the French Army going on to establish a dedicated training school in 1852. Inspired by these visits, Hamilton's report concluded with a strong recommendation for the British Army to adopt gymnastics training.[10]

Based on this recommendation, in 1860, Major Frederick Hammersely of the 14th Regiment of Foot took twelve carefully selected senior non-commissioned officers (referred to by the Royal Army Physical Training Corps as the 'Twelve Apostles') from various regiments in the British Army to Oxford. Here they attended an intensive six-month course in gymnastics, under the supervision of Archibald McLaren at the Oxford University Gymnasium. McLaren was an early pioneer of sport science, and would produce the book *A Military System of Gymnastic Exercises for the Use of Instructors* in 1862, which featured many of the techniques learned by the Twelve Apostles. This training was aimed at developing muscular strength, so the 'Twelve Apostles' mostly worked on the trapeze, with horizontal and parallel bars and with heavy dumb-bells. In the age of the strongman, their training successfully achieved its aim of increasing upper-body strength but resulted in comparatively inadequate lower-body support.

Major Hammersley would later go on to become the first Inspector of Gymnasia, and the success of this programme led, in 1861, to the first gymnasium being built at Wellington Lines in Aldershot, and, from 1862, a gymnasium to be built in every garrison. The 'Twelve Apostles' were posted out to garrisons at home and abroad to train others to become instructors in their own regiments, and the Army Gymnastic Staff came into being.

As early as 1865, physical training regulations were published stipulating that physical training should take precedence over all other training in the first two months of a recruit's service. Recruits now had to carry out one hour of physical training per day in order to pass certain tests. Those showing the most aptitude in their three-month annual training course were selected for a further three-month course at Aldershot. The best of these were then selected for the Gymnastic Staff.

The course at Aldershot focused mainly on training with dumb-bells, barbells, climbing ropes, vaulting horse and horizontal bars. There were also various beams and ropes set up outside for balancing exercise in full equipment, as well as areas for practicing boxing, fencing and single-stick fighting. All of this was done in the gymnastic kit of full uniform minus the jacket. In 1876, Major Gildea succeeded Major Hammersley as Inspector of Gymnasia and in 1878 presented an 'Assault-at Arms' at the Royal Albert Hall, which proved so successful it grew into what is now widely known as the Royal Tournament.

In 1885, the Army Gymnastic Staff were, for the first time, officially recognised in the Army List, under the general heading of 'Schools of Instruction'. The value of physical training was increasing more and more during this period, and with the appointment of Colonel Fox as Inspector for Gymnasia in 1890 it grew even further.

Colonel Fox was responsible for many of the buildings used across the country for physical training, such as the new Headquarters Gymnasium (initially named the Cranbrook Gymnasium, later renamed Fox Gymnasium), which was built at Aldershot in 1894 to cater for the increasing number of applicants to the course. It was also during this time that the Army Gymnastic Staff undertook bayonet training in addition to their existing physical training, gymnastics, boxing and fencing.

In 1890, Colonel Fox had visited Sweden and was very impressed with their system of training, which had been in place for 100 years and was used throughout the Scandinavian armies. This was the 'Ling System', which involved moving away from an upper-body muscle-building programme to an all-over-body fitness. Colonel Fox tried to convince the War Office of its benefits, but they believed it would be too difficult to teach without additional academic training so rejected the idea. They did, however, allow the introduction of a free gymnastics system in 1894–5, which was an improvement on earlier techniques. This system remained until 1906, when Lieutenant Lankilda, of the Danish Army, arrived in Aldershot to introduce the Army Gymnastic Staff to the 'Ling System'. The gymnasiums were immediately refurbished to reduce the number of dumb-bells, horizontal bars and parallel bars in favour of balancing beams and wall bars.

Colonel Fox was succeeded by Colonel Napier in 1897. He was able to complete and extend what Colonel Fox had started. Colonel Napier increased the number of gymnasia built to over eighty throughout the country and so doubled the number of staff employed. Galleries in the gymnasium at Aldershot were added to allow people to watch the boxing competitions and other displays.

However, Colonel Napier's lasting legacy in Aldershot was the swimming pool that is still located on Fox Lines. He was the first person to advocate the inclusion of swimming in the training programme as a way to keep the soldiers both fit and happy, but as there was no Army funding for this project he had to find the resources to build the swimming pool himself.

At the outbreak of war in 1914, the majority of the warrant officers and senior non-commissioned officers serving with the Army Gymnastic Staff were returned to their original units. The War Office quickly realised the error it had made and issued orders to reform a new staff; the outbreak of the First World War had signalled an unprecedented upturn in the number of recruits requiring training. The Inspector of Gymnasia in 1914, Colonel Wright, managed to assemble 180 non-commissioned officer instructors at Aldershot by the start of September. Colonel Wright had the joint problems of having to be able to train enough instructors to cater for the new demand and also having to adapt the established training styles to the circumstances of war.[11]

2

The 'Yellow Peril': Manual of Physical Training, 1908 and NCO's Table Card, 1908

The first official *Manual of Physical Training* embodying the modern style of physical training known as the 'Ling' or 'Swedish' System was published in 1908. Major Charles Moore, Assistant Inspector, was responsible for publishing the manual, which became known as the 'Yellow Peril' due to its mustard-yellow cover and the apprehension of soldiers towards the daunting physical exercises that it contained. The manual was, however, a complete success, and held in such high regard in Holland that it was translated into Dutch.[1] A selection of its pages, including arm and abdominal exercises, is included in this chapter.

The 'Table Cards' provided details of a series of exercises at various levels of difficulty. Peacetime tables for recruits contained exercises that totalled 110 hours, to be carried out for one hour per day, five days per week.[2] The level of time spent on each of the exercise tables differed depending on the individual progression of each recruit, however it would be expected that, after each table had been completed seven to ten times, the recruit would progress to the next table of exercise. The tables would increase in difficulty: table one would be easier than table two, while table three would be more difficult and provide a greater challenge than table two. The tables were designed to allow a certain degree of flexibility when carrying out each exercise, for instance those activities that required the use of particular equipment could be substituted for another exercise (lateral, abdominal and dorsal exercises could be interchanged); this was necessary because apparatus and space would be limited when a large group of men were under instruction at the same time. The 1908 NCO's Table Card reproduced here was to be used for those under instruction at the Headquarters Gymnasium at Aldershot, but additional table cards were developed for training infantry, cavalry and artillery recruits, along with trained soldiers.

N.C.O.'s TABLE CARD

CONTAINING

Tables of Exercises

FOR

NON-COMMISSIONED OFFICERS UNDER TRAINING

AT THE

Head Quarter Gymnasium, Aldershot.

Issued June, 1908.

(B 1973) Wt. w. 3745—z.1./95/2*a* 500 11/12 H & S

N.C.O.'s PHYSICAL TRAINING TABLES.

—◆—

1. The following Tables are intended for use during the N.C.O.'s course of Instruction at the Head Quarter Gymnasium, Aldershot. They represent the actual daily exercise of the N.C.O.'s under instruction in accordance with the Army system of Physical Training and should be taken in such a way as to ensure the fullest physical benefit from the work.

2. The period of time during which each N.C.O.'s Table is used must depend on progress, but as a rule it should be for about a week of 5 attendances.

SYLLABUS OF INSTRUCTION
during the four months' course at the Head Quarter Gymnasium, Aldershot.

———◆———

1. **Practical instruction** in the exercises comprised in N.C.O.'s, Recruits' and Trained Soldiers' Tables.

2. **Class-taking.**—Giving words of command, arrangement of apparatus, method of handling a class, explanation and illustration of exercises, detection and correction of errors, use of the Tables, employment of *complementary*, *supplementary leg* and *corrective* exercises.

3. **Theory.**—Object and scope of physical training, principles and application of the system, object and application of the various exercises, elementary anatomy and physiology and their application to physical training, formation of classes and conduct of physical training and exercise, hygiene as applied to physical training, regulations concerning physical training and exercise.

4. **Bayonet Fighting (Swordsmanship** for Cavalry N.C.O.'s)—Giving and taking lessons, the Assault, R.N. & M.T. rules for individual and team fighting, judging competition fighting.

5. **Swimming.**

ABBREVIATIONS, etc.

A.	= Arm or Arms.	K.	= Knee or Knees
A.b.	= Arms bend.	K.b.	= Knees bend.
Abd.	= Abdominal.	L.	= Leg or Legs.
astr.	= astride.	Lat.	= Lateral.
backw.	= backward.	Mar.	= Marching.
Bal.	= Balance.	N.	= Neck.
b.	= bend or bending.	N.r.	= Neck rest.
cl.	= close or closing.	o.	= open.
Cor.	= Corrective.	oblique gr.	
crossgr.	= crossgrip.		= oblique grip.
Dor.	= Dorsal.	outw.	= outward.
downw.	= downward.	overgr.	= overgrip.
F.	= Foot or Feet.	pl.	= place or placing.
ex.	= exercise.	pos.	= position.
F.cl.	= Feet close.	r.	= raise or raising.
F.full o.	= Feet full open.	sidew.	= sideways.
f.	= firm.	sit.	= sitting.
fling.	= flinging.	Sp. b.	= Span bending.
forw.	= forward.	str.	= stretch or stretch-
H.	= Hips.		ing.
hang.	= hanging.	swg.	= swing or swinging.
H.f.	= Hips firm.	Tr.	= Trunk.
Hl.	= Heels.	turn.	= turning.
Hl.r.	= Heels raise.	upw.	= upward.
Hvg.	= Heaving.	undergr.	= under grip.
inw.	= inward.	V.	= Vaulting.
J.	= Jumping.		

(i.) Parts of the body and names of the groups of exercises are commenced with a Capital letter, all other words with a small letter.

(ii.) The starting positions, when entailing more than one movement in order to obtain them, are written in the order in which the movements are commanded; when these movements are taken separately a comma is used between each, but when taken together no comma is used and the order of the movements is given from the feet upwards

(iii.) In the Tables a dash — is used between the starting position and the exercise, and the name of the exercise (including any additional movements taken to increase the effect) is given in **thick type.**

(iv.) When there is any possibility of doubt as to whether one or both Arms, Legs, Knees, etc., are meant, an "s" is added to the abbreviation when both limbs are referred to, or the figure 1 is used if only one is intended.

N.C.O.'s TABLE I.

A.—INTRODUCTORY EXERCISES.

1. L. ex.   (a.) **Feet close.**
            (b.) **Heels raise.**
2. N. ex.   **Head bending backward.**
3. A. ex.   (a.) **Hips firm.**
            (b.) **Arms bend,** and add later—
            (c.) A.b.—**Arms sideways stretch.**
4. Tr. ex.   F.cl., H.f.—**Trunk turning.**
5. L. ex.   (a.) H.f., Hl.r.—**Knees bend.**
            (b.) H.f.—**Foot sideways place.**

B.—GENERAL EXERCISES.

1. Preparation   **Feet astride Arms upward stretch.**
   for Sp.b.   (Taken "free").
2. Hvg. ex. (a.) **Fall hanging.** (Beam Breast high,
                 down to Waist high), and add later—
                 Fall hang.—**Arms bend.**
            (b.) **Arch hanging.**
3. Bal. ex. (a.) H.f.—**Knee raising.**
            (b.) **Mounting beam** (under Knee height).
4. Lat. ex.   F.cl., H.f.—**Trunk bending side-
                 ways.**
5. Abd. ex.   H.f., F. sidew. pl. — **Trunk bending
                 backward.**
6. Dor. ex.   H.f., F. sidew. pl. — **Trunk bending
                 forward.**
7. Mar. ex. (a.) **Quick March . . . . Halt.**
            (b.) **Double March . . . . Halt.**
            (c.) **Quick mark time . . . Halt.**
8. Hvg. ex. (a.) **Overgrip.**
            (b.) **Crossgrip.**
9. J. & V. (a.) **Upward jumping.**
            (b.) **Downward jumping.**
            (c.) Beam grasp—**First position.**
            (d.) **Class arrangements for jumping
                 over rope.** And add later—
            (e.) **Jumping over rope with run**
                 (taken "free").
            (f.) **Long jumping over two chalk lines.**

C.—FINAL EXERCISES.

1. L. ex.   **Heels raise.**
2. Cor. ex. **Arms raising sideways.**

A.—INTRODUCTORY EXERCISES.

1. L. ex.		H.f. — Heels raising **and Knees** bending.
2. N. ex.		**Head bending backward.**
3. A. ex.	(*a.*)	A.b.—**Arms sideways stretch.**
	(*b.*)	A.b.—**Arms upward stretch.**
4. Tr. ex.		H.f., F. sidew. pl.—**Trunk turning.**
5. L. ex.		H.f.—**Feet astride place.**

B.—GENERAL EXERCISES.

1. Preparation for Sp. b.		F. astr. A. upw. str. (taken "free").— **Trunk bending backward** (slight movement only).
2. Hvg. ex.	(*a.*)	**Fall** hang.—**Arms bend.** (Beam Waist high.)
	(*b.*)	Fall hang.—**Leg raising.**
	(*c.*)	Arch hang.—**Arms bend.**
3. Bal. ex.	(*a.*)	H.f.—**Leg raising sideways.**
	(*b.*)	**Walking forward on beam.** (Up to Knee height.)
4. Lat. ex.		H.f., F. sidew. pl. — **Trunk bending sideways.**
5. Abd. ex.	(*a.*)	**On the Hands** (on bench) and add later **Arms bend.**
	(*b.*)	Lying, A. upw. r.—**Leg raising.**
6. Dor. ex.		H.f., F. sidew. pl. — **Trunk forward bend.** and add later,— A.b., F. sidew. pl. — **Trunk forward bend.**
7. Mar. ex.		As before and—
	(*d.*)	Quick march—**Heels raise.**
	(*e.*)	Running—**Long stride.**
8. Hvg. ex.	(*a.*)	**Oblique grip.**
	(*b.*)	**Under grip.**
9. J. & V.	(*a.*) & (*b.*)	as before.
	(*c.*)	**Forward jumping.**
	(*d.*)	**With 3 paces forward off the left Foot jump.**
	(*e.*)	With run—**First position.**
	(*f.*)	**On the Knees** (without run).
	(*g.*)	**On the Feet to Attention** without run (box and pommel horse).

C.—FINAL EXERCISES.

1. L. ex.	H.f.—**Foot placing sideways.**
2. Cor. ex.	**Arms raising sideways.**

N.C.O.'s TABLE III.

A.—INTRODUCTORY EXERCISES.

1. L. ex.   H.f. — Heels raising and Knees bending.
2. N. ex.   Head turning.
3. A. ex.   (a.) A.b.—Arms stretching sideways.
               (b.) A.b.—Left Arm upward right Arm downward stretch.
4. Tr. ex.   H.f., F. sidew. pl. —Trunk turning quickly.
5. L. ex.   Feet astride Arms upward stretch.

B.—GENERAL EXERCISES.

1. Preparation for Sp.b.   F. astr. A. upw. str.—Trunk bending backward.
               (H.f., F. astr.—Trunk bending forward and downward).
2. Hvg. ex.   (a.) Crossgr.—Arms bend.
               (b.) Overgr.—Side travelling.
3. Bal. ex.   (a.) H.f.—Leg raising backward.
               (b.) Turning about on beam. (Up to Knee height.)
4. Lat. ex.   On the Hands—On the left Hand turn (on bench), and add Leg raising.
5. Abd. ex.   (a.) On the Hands—Arms bend (on bench).
               (b.) Lying, A. upw. r.—Legs raising.
6. Dor. ex.   Forw. lying—Hips firm (on bench).
7. Mar. ex.   As before and—
               (f.) Change step.
8. Hvg. ex.   Position for climbing.
9. J. & V.   Free standing jumps as before and—
               (e.) Jumping over rope with 3 paces forward off the left Foot.
               (f.) Long jumping with 3 paces forward off the left Foot.
               (g.) Upward jumping with Arms raising sideways.
               (h.) On the Feet to Attention with run (box and pommel horse).
               (i.) On the Feet to astride position without run (pommel horse).

C.—FINAL EXERCISES.

1. L. ex.   H.f.—Foot placing sideways.
2. Tr. ex.   H.f., F. sidew. pl.—Trunk bending sideways.
3. Cor. ex.   Arms raising sideways.

N.C.O.'s TABLE IV.

A.—INTRODUCTORY EXERCISES.

1. L. ex.   H.f.—**Foot placing sideways.**
2. N. ex.   **Head turning.**
3. A. ex.   (*a.*) A.b.—**Arms stretching upward.**
          (*b.*) A. sidew. r.—**Arms forward bend,** and add later **Arms flinging.**
4. Tr. ex.   A.b., F. sidew. pl. — **Trunk bending forward,** and add later **Arms stretching sideways.**
5. L. ex.   H.f. — **Heels raising and Knees bending quickly.**

B.—GENERAL EXERCISES.

1. Sp. b.   **Position for Span bending** (taken "free" with F. astr. ; and later by word of command).
2. Hvg. ex. (*a.*) Undergr.—**Arms bend.**
          (*b.*) Repetition as required.
3. Bal. ex. (*a.*) H.f., K.r.—**Leg forward stretch.**
          (*b.*) **Mounting beam with run.** (Up to Hip height.)
4. Lat. ex. (*a.*) F.cl., 1 A.upw. 1 A.downw.str. — **Trunk bending sideways.**
          (*b.*) On the left Hand – **Leg raising.** (On bench.)
5. Abd. ex.   **On the Hands** (on ground), and add later **Arms bend.**
6. Dor. ex.   Forw. lying, H.f. — **Trunk bending backward.**
7. Mar. ex. As before.
8. Hvg. ex. **Climbing.**
9. J. & V.   Free standing jumps and jumping over rope as before and—

             Upward jumping (2 or 3 jumps without pause).
      (*h.*) **On the top bar up.**
      (*i.*) **Vault with Foot assisting.**
      (*j.*) **On the Feet to Attention or to astride position with feint** (pommel horse).
      (*k.*) **On the Feet to Attention and splits off** and later **On the Feet and splits off** (box horse lengthways).
      (*l.*) **Mounting pommel horse** (cavalry horse).

C.—FINAL EXERCISES.

1. L. ex.   **Feet close and Feet open** (counting 6 or more beats).
2. Tr. ex.   F. cl., H.f.—**Trunk turning.**
3. Cor. ex.   **Arms raising sideways.**

A.—INTRODUCTORY EXERCISES.

1. L. ex.   H.f.—Foot placing sideways.
2. N. ex.   Head turning quickly.
3. A. ex.   Arms swinging upward.
4. Tr. ex.   H.f., F. sidew. pl. — **Trunk bending sideways quickly.**
5. L. ex.   H.f.—**Heels raising and Knees bending.**

B.—GENERAL EXERCISES.

1. Sp. b.   Pos. for Sp. b. (F. astr.)—**Heels raise.** (1 foot-length from wall bars.)
2. Hvg. ex.   (a.) Oblique gr.—**Arms bend.**
               (b.) Repetition as required.
3. Bal. ex.   (a.) H.f.—**Leg raising forward.**
               (b.) **Walking forward on beam.** (Hip height.)
4. Lat. ex.   (a.) On the Hands—**On the left Hand turn.** (At wall bars.)
               (b.) Sit. astr., H.f.—**Trunk turning.**
5. Abd. ex.   (a.) On the Hands—**Arms bend** (on ground).
               (b.) F. support, H.f. — **Trunk bending backward.**
6. Dor. ex.   (a.) F. astr. A. upw. str.—**Trunk bending forward.**
               (b.) Forw. lying, H.f. — **Trunk bending backward.**
7. Mar. ex.   As before and—
               (g.) H.f.—**With Knee raising quick mark time.**
8. Hvg. ex.   **Side travelling from rope to rope.**
9. J. & V.   Free standing jumps and jumping over rope as required.
               (h.) **Combined high and long jump.**
               (i.) **Heaving jump** (side to beam).
               (j.) **Running over and under skipping rope.**
               (k.) **Between the pommels** without run (pommel horse).
               (l.) **On the Feet and off** with run (box horse).
               (m.) **Left Hand Vault.**

C.—FINAL EXERCISES.

1. L. ex.   **H.f.—Heels raising and Knees bending quickly.**
2. Tr. ex.   **A.b., F. sidew. pl.— Trunk bending forward.**
3. Cor. ex.   **Arms raising sideways.**

N.C.O.'s TABLE VI.

A.—INTRODUCTORY EXERCISES.

1. L. ex.   H.f.—Foot placing sideways.
2. N. ex.   Head bending backward.
3. A. ex.   Arms swinging upward.
4. Tr. ex.   H.f., F. sidew. pl. — Trunk bending
                forward.
5. L. ex.   H.f.—Heels raising and full Knees
                bending.

B.—GENERAL EXERCISES.

1. Sp.b.   Pos. for Sp. b. (F. astr.)—Heels raise. (2
                foot-lengths from wall bars).
2. Hvg. ex.   (a.) Oblique gr.—Backward travelling
                (b.) Undergr.—Upward circling.
                (c.) Repetition as required.
3. Bal. ex.   (a.) H.f.—Leg raising forward.
                (b.) Walking backward on beam (up to
                Hip height).
4. Lat. ex.   On the left Hand—Leg raising. (At wall
                bars.)
5. Abd. ex.   (a.) On the Hands (on ground)—Feet placing
                forward.
                (b.) Overgr. — Knees raising. (Wall bars or
                beam).
6. Dor. ex.   Forw. lying, H.f. — Trunk bending
                forward.
7. Mar. ex.   As before and—
                (h.) Slow march.
8. Hvg. ex.   Upward and downward travelling
                from rope to rope.
9. J. & V.   Free standing jumps and jumping over rope
                as required and—
                Upward jumping with turning.
                (h.) Heaving jump (side to beam) 2 jumps.
                (i.) Repetition of vaults on box and pommel horse.
                (j.) Splits over lengthways (box and pommel
                horse).
                (k.) Skipping rope.
                (l.) Hurdle over benches.
                (m.) Quick run along benches.

C.—FINAL EXERCISES.

1. L. ex.   H.f.—Heels raising and Knees bend
                ing quickly.
2. Tr. ex.   H.f., F. astr. — Trunk bending back
                ward.
3. A. ex.   A. forw. b.—Arms flinging.
4. Cor. ex.   Head bending backward.

A.—INTRODUCTORY EXERCISES.

1. L. ex.   H.f.—**Heels raising and Knees bend-ing quickly.**
2. N. ex.   **Head turning.**
3. A. ex.   A. upw. str.—**Arms swinging down-ward and backward.**
4. Tr. ex.   A. upw. str.—**Trunk bending backward.**
5. L. ex.   (a.) **Feet astride Arms sideways stretch.**
                   (b.) **Feet astride Arms bend.**

B.—GENERAL EXERCISES.

1. Sp.b.   Pos. for Sp. b. (F. astr.) — **Heels raise.** (2 foot-lengths from wall bars).
2. Hvg. ex.   (a.) **Twisting to sitting position,** and add la er **Twisting about.**
                   (b.) Overgr. – **Side travelling changing grip.**
3. Bal. ex.   **Turning about on beam** (up to Hip height).
4. Lat. ex.   H.f., F. support.—**Trunk bending side-ways.**
5. Abd. ex.   **On the Hands** (Feet on bench or beam).
6. Dor. ex.   Forw. lying, H.f.—**Trunk bending back-ward and forward.**
7. Mar. ex.   As before and:—
                   (i.) H.f.—**With Knee raising quick march.**
8. Hvg. ex.   (a.) Overgr.—**Side travelling with swing.**
                   (b.) Repetition as required.
9. J. & V.   Free standing jumps and jumping over rope, etc., as required.
                   Previous vaults on horse, etc., as required and—
                   (h.) **Between the Hands** with run (pommel and box horse).
                   (i.) **Mounting shelf with assistance and circling down.**
                   (j.) **Double beam** (over, under and between, moving "free").

C.—FINAL EXERCISES.

1. L. ex.   H.f.—**Heels raising and full Knees bending.**
2. Tr. ex.   F. astr. H.f.—**Trunk turning.**
3. Cor. ex.   **Arms raising sideways and up-ward.**

A.—INTRODUCTORY EXERCISES.

1.	L. ex.	H.f.—**Foot placing sideways.**
2.	N. ex.	Head bending **sideways.**
3.	A. ex.	A.b.—**Arms stretching sideways and upward.**
4.	Tr. ex.	A. upw. str. — **Trunk bending backward.**
5.	L. ex.	H.f.—**Heels raising and full Knees bending quickly.**

B.—GENERAL EXERCISES.

1.	Sp.b.	Pos. for Sp. b. (F. astr.) — **Heels raise** (2 foot-lengths from wall bars).
2.	Hvg. ex.	(*a.*) Overgr.—**Side travelling with swing.**
		(*b.*) Crossgr., A.b.—**Backward travelling.**
3.	Bal. ex.	(*a.*) H f.—**Leg raising backward.**
		(*b.*) **Mounting beam** (from Hip to Shoulder height).
4.	Lat. ex.	F. support, 1 A. upw. 1 Hand H. f.—**Trunk bending sideways.**
5.	Abd. ex.	**On** the Hands — **Leg raising.** (On ground).
		And add later —
		On the Hands, A.b.—**Leg raising.** (On ground).
6.	Dor. ex.	Forw. lying, A.b.—**Trunk bending backward and forward.**
7.	Mar. ex.	**As before.**
8.	Hvg. ex.	**Twisting passing each other.**
9.	J. & V.	Repetition of previous J. &. V. exercises as required and—
		(*h.*) **Splits over pommels** with run (pommel horse).
		(*i.*) **Jumping over rope with 3 paces forward off the left Foot landing in chalked circle.**
		(*j.*) **Both ranks mounting shelf with assistance and downward jumping.**
		(*k.*) **Combined obstacles** (Hurdle over benches—Double beam—Running along benches—and return).

C.—FINAL EXERCISES.

1.	L. ex.	A.b.—**Heels raising.**
2.	Tr. ex.	H.f., F. sidew. pl. — **Trunk bending sideways.**
3.	Cor. ex.	**Arms raising sideways and upward.**

N.C.O.'s TABLE IX.

A.—INTRODUCTORY EXERCISES.

1. L. ex.		A.b.—**Heels** raising **and** Knees **bending.**
2. N. ex.		**Head bending sideways.**
3. A. ex.		A. upw. str.—**Arms swinging downward and backward.**
4. Tr. ex.		F. astr. A. sidew. str.—**Trunk bending sideways.**
5. L. ex.	(*a.*)	H.f., F.cl.—**Feet full open.**
	(*b.*)	H.f., F. full o.—**Foot outward place.**

B.—GENERAL EXERCISES.

1. Sp. b.		Pos. for Sp. b. (Hl together).—**Heels raise** (2 foot-lengths from wall bars).
2. Hvg. ex.	(*a.*)	Fall hang., A.b.—**Leg raising.**
	(*b.*)	**Changing between arch hanging and fall hanging.**
3. Bal. ex.		**Walking forward on beam** (from Hip to Shoulder height).
4. Lat. ex.		On the Hands—**On the left Hand turn.** (On ground.)
5. Abd. ex.		Sit., H.f.—**Trunk bending backward** (45°).
6. Dor. ex.	(*a.*)	Forw. lying, A.b., Tr. backw. (forw.) b.—**Arms stretching sideways.**
	(*b.*)	F. astr. A. upw. str.—**Trunk bending forward.**
7. Mar. ex.		As before—
8. Hvg. ex.	(*a.*)	Undergr.—**Arms bend.**
	(*b.*)	Oblique gr.—**Arms bend.**
9. J. & V.		Repetition of previous J. & V. exercises as required and—
	(*h.*)	**Heaving jump** (facing beam).
	(*i.*)	**Vault over double beam.**
	(*j.*)	**Scissors** (horse lengthways).
	(*k.*)	**Mounting wall with assistance from below.**
	(*l.*)	**Obstacle training** (repetition).

C.—FINAL EXERCISES.

1. L. ex.	H.f.—**Heels raising and full Knees bending.**
2. Tr. ex.	H.f., F. sidew. pl.—**Trunk bending backward.**
3. Cor. ex.	**Arms raising sideways and upward.**

N.C.O.'s TABLE X.

A.—INTRODUCTORY EXERCISES.

1. L. ex.	H.f., F. full o.—**Foot placing outward.**
2. N. ex.	**Head bending backward.**
3. A. ex.	A.b.—**Arms stretching sideways and upward.** (Twice in each direction.)
4. Tr. ex.	A.b., F. sidew. pl.—**Trunk turning.**
5. L. ex.	H.f., F. full o.—**Outward lunge.**

B.—GENERAL EXERCISES.

1. Sp. b.	Pos. for Sp. b. (Hl. together)—**Heels raise** (2 foot-lengths from wall bars).
2. Hvg. ex.	(a.) **Climbing both Hands leading with the Feet.**
	(b.) Oblique gr. — **Backward travelling with Arms bending between each pace.**
3. Bal. ex.	**Turning about on beam** (up to Shoulder height).
4. Lat. ex.	(a.) F. astr. A. sidew. str.—**Trunk bending sideways quickly.**
	(b.) On the left Hand—**Leg raising.** (On ground).
5. Abd. ex.	Sit., H.f.—**Trunk bending backward.**
6. Dor. ex.	F. astr. A. upw. str., Tr. forw. b.—**Arms swinging downward and backward.**
7. Mar. ex.	**As** before and—
	(f.) **On alternate Feet hop.**
8. Hvg. ex.	**Climbing inclined rope.**
9. J. & V.	Repetition of previous J. & **V. exercises** as required and—
	(h.) **Horizontal vault.**
	(i.) **Heaving jump with rope** (combined high and long jump).
	(j.) **Mounting wall with assistance from above.**
	(k.) **Obstacle training** (repetition and obstacle course).

C.—FINAL EXERCISES.

1. L. ex.	H.f.—**Heels raising and full Knees bending.**
2. Tr. ex.	H.f., F. sidew. pl. — **Trunk bending forward.**
3. Cor. ex.	**Arms raising sideways and upward.**

A.—INTRODUCTORY EXERCISES.

1. L. ex.	}	H.f. (and later A.b.), full K.b. — **Head turning quickly.**
2. N. ex.		
3. A. ex.		A.upw. str.—**Arms swinging downward and backward.**
4. Tr. ex.	(a.)	A.b.,F.astr.—**Trunk bending backward.**
	(b.)	A.b., F. astr.—**Trunk bending forward.**
5. L. ex.	(a.)	H.f.—**Foot forward place.**
	(b.)	A.b., F. full o.—**Lunging outward.**

B.—GENERAL EXERCISES.

1. Sp.b.		**Fall hanging to Span bending.** (Beam breast high.) (A. upw. str., F. sidew. pl.—**Trunk bending forward and downward.**)
2. Hvg. ex.	(a.)	Oblique gr.—**Backward travelling with Arms bending between each pace.**
	(b.)	**Climbing inclined rope.**
3. Bal. ex.	(a.)	H.f.—**Leg raising forward sideways and backward.**
	(b.)	**Mounting beam** (over Shoulder height).
4. Lat. ex.		A.b., F. sidew. pl., Tr. turn.— **Arms stretching upward.**
5. Abd. ex.	(a.)	Overgr.—**Legs raising.**
	(b.)	Sit., A.b.—**Trunk bending backward.**
6. Dor. ex.	(a.)	F. full o., H.f. (and later A.b.) — **Toe support backward lunge.**
7. Mar. ex.		As before and—
	(k.)	**On the left Foot hop.**
	(l.)	H.f.—**With Knee raising double march.**
8. Hvg. ex.		Overgr.—**Arms bend** (with assistance).
9. J. & V.		Repetition of previous J. & V. exercises as required and—
	(h.)	**Bent backlift** (pommel and box horse and parallels).
	(i.)	**Heaving jump** (from box horse).
	(j.)	**Hopping with Leg raising sideways.**
	(k.)	**Jumping over rope with oblique run.**
	(d.)	**Obstacle training** (repetition).

C.—FINAL EXERCISES.

1. L. ex.	H.f., F. full o.—**Foot placing outward.**
2. Tr. ex.	F. cl., H.f.—**Trunk bending sideways.**
3. Cor. ex.	**Arms raising forward upward sideways and downward.**

N.C.O.'s TABLE XII.

A.—INTRODUCTORY EXERCISES.

1. L. ex.		H.f.—**Foot placing forward.**
2. N. ex.		**Head bending forward.**
3. A. ex.		A.b.—**Arms forward stretch.**
4. Tr. ex.	(a.)	F. astr. A. upw. str., Tr. forw. b.—**Arms swinging downward and backward.**
	(b.)	H.f., F. outw. pl.—**Trunk turning.**
5. L. ex.		A.b., full K.b.—**Arms stretching sideways.**

B.—GENERAL EXERCISES.

1. Sp.b.		Pos. for Sp. b. (Hl. together)—(a.) **Knee raising,** (b.) **Heels raising.**
2. Hvg. ex.	(a.)	Overgr.—**Arms bend.**
	(b.)	**Climbing inclined rope with turning.**
3. Bal. ex.	(a.)	**Leg raising forward sideways and backward with Arms raising forward sideways and upward.**
	(b.)	**Walking forward on beam** (over Shoulder height).
4. Lat. ex.		A.b., F. full o.—**Lunging outward with one Arm upward one Arm downward stretching.**
5. Ald. ex.	(a.)	Overgr., Ks.r.—**Leg forward stretch.**
	(b.)	Sit., A. upw. str.—**Trunk bending backward.**
6. Dor. ex.	(a.)	A.b., Toe support backw. lunge. — **Arms stretching sideways,** and later **Arms stretching upward.**
	(b.)	Forw. lying, A.b., Tr. backw. b. — **Arms stretching upward.**
7. Mar. ex.		As before and—
	(m.)	H.f.—**In quick time sideways to the left march.**
8. Hvg. ex.		Repeat **Climbing inclined rope with turning,** or as required.
9. J. & V.		Repetition of previous J. & V. exercises as required and—
	(h.)	**With turning one (three) paces forward off the left Foot jump.**
	(i.)	**Leg swingings** (pommel horse).
	(j.)	**Obstacle training** (repetition and racing).

C.—FINAL EXERCISES.

1. L. ex.		H.f., F. full o.—**Foot placing outward.**
2. Tr. ex.		H.f., F. outw. pl.—**Trunk turning.**
3. Cor. ex.		**Arms raising forward upward sideways and downward.**

N.C.O.'s TABLE XIII.

A.—INTRODUCTORY EXERCISES.

1. L. ex.		**H.f.—Foot placing sideways and Heels raising.**
2. N. ex.		**Head bending backward.**
3. A. ex.	(a.)	**A.b.—Arms stretching forward and sideways.**
	(b.)	**Neck rest.**
4. Tr. ex.	(a.)	H.f., F. forw. pl.—**Trunk bending backward.**
	(b.)	H.f., F. forw. pl.—**Trunk bending forward.**
5. L. ex.		**Heels raising and Knees bending quickly with Arms stretching upward.**

B.—GENERAL EXERCISES.

1. Sp.b.	Pos. for Sp.b. (Hl. together). Hl. r.—**Knee raising**, and later Hl.r., K.r.—**Leg forward stretch.**
2. Hvg. ex.	Undergr., A.b.—**Side travelling.**
3. Bal. ex.	H.f., etc.—**Walking forward on beam with Knee raising.**
4. Lat. ex.	F. astr. A. upw. str. — **Trunk bending sideways.**
5. Abd. ex.	Sit., A.b., Tr. backw. b.—**Arms stretching upward.**
6. Dor. ex.	(a.) Forw. lying, A.b., Tr. backw. b. — **Arms stretching upward.**
	(b.) F. support, H.f.—**Lunging forward.**
7. Mar. ex.	As before and—
	(n.) H.f.—**In double time sideways to the left march.**
8. Hvg. ex.	Repetition as required.
9. J. & V.	Repetition as required and—
	Upward jumping with Arms swinging upward.

C.—FINAL EXERCISES.

1. L. ex.	H.f., F. full o.—**Lunging forward.**
2. Tr. ex.	H.f., F. forw. pl.—**Trunk turning.**
3. Cor. ex.	**Heels raising.**

N.C.O.'s TABLE XIV.

A.—INTRODUCTORY EXERCISES.

1. L. ex.   H.f.—**Foot placing sideways and Heels raising and Knees bending.**
2. N. ex.   **Head turning quickly.**
3. A. ex.   A.b.—**Arms stretching sideways with palms up and Arms raising upward.**
4. Tr. ex.   (*a.*) F. astr. A.b., Tr. (slightly) backw. b.— **Arms stretching upward.**
           (*b.*) N.r., F.cl.—**Trunk turning.**
5. L. ex.   A. forw. b.—**Foot placing sideways with Arms flinging.**

B.—GENERAL EXERCISES.

1. Sp.b.   Pos. for Sp. b. (Hl. together), Hl.r.—**Leg raising.**
2. Hvg. ex.   Oblique gr., A.b.—**Backward travelling.**
3. Bal. ex.   **Walking backward on beam.**
4. Lat. ex.   H. support, 1 A. upw. 1 Hand H.f.— **Trunk bending sideways with Leg raising.**
5. Abd. ex.   On the Hands—**Arm forward and upward raise.**
6. Dor. ex.   (*a.*) F. astr. A. upw. str., Tr. forw. b.—**Arms swinging downward and backward.**
           (*b.*) F. support, A.h., forw. lunge — **Arms stretching sideways (upward).**
7. Mar. ex.   As before.
8. Hvg. ex.   Repetition as required and—
           Overgr., A.b.—**Side travelling.**
9. J. & V.   Repetition as required.

C.—FINAL EXERCISES.

1. L. ex.   N.r.—**Heels raising and full Knees bending.**
2. Tr. ex.   N.r., F.cl. — **Trunk bending sideways.**
3. Cor. ex.   **Arms raising sideways with Heels raising.**

MANUAL

OF

PHYSICAL TRAINING.

(Reprint 1908 with Amendments published in Army Orders
to 1st December, 1914.)

LONDON:
PRINTED UNDER THE AUTHORITY OF HIS MAJESTY'S STATIONERY OFFICE
By HARRISON AND SONS, 45-47, St. Martin's Lane, W.C.,
Printers in Ordinary to His Majesty.

To be purchased, either directly or through any Bookseller, from
WYMAN AND SONS, Ltd., 29, Breams Buildings, Fetter Lane E.C., and
54, St, Mary Street, Cardiff; or
H.M. STATIONERY OFFICE (Scottish Branch), 23, Forth Street, Edinburgh; or
E. PONSONBY, Ltd., 116, Grafton Street, Dublin;
or from the Agencies in the British Colonies and Dependencies,
the United States of America, the Continent of Europe and Abroad of
T. FISHER UNWIN, London, W.C.

1914.

Price Ninepence.

SECTION IV.

ABBREVIATIONS, NOMENCLATURE, EXPLANATION OF TERMS USED.

ABBREVIATIONS.

46.

A.	= Arm or Arms.	H.	= Hips.
A. b.	= Arms bend.	hang.	= hanging.
Abd.	= Abdominal.	H. f.	= Hips firm.
astr.	= astride.	Hl.	= Heels.
backw.	= backward.	Hl. r.	= Heels raise.
Bal.	= Balance.	Hvg.	= Heaving.
b.	= bend or bending.	inw.	= inward.
cl.	= close or closing.	J.	= Jumping.
Cor.	= Corrective.	K.	= Knee or Knees.
crossgr.	= crossgrip.	K. b.	= Knees bend.
Dor.	= Dorsal.	L.	= Leg or Legs.
downw.	= downward.	Lat.	= Lateral.
F.	= Foot or Feet.	Mar.	= Marching.
ex.	= exercise.	N.	= Neck.
F. cl.	= Feet close.	N. r.	= Neck rest.
F. full o.	= Feet full open.	o.	= open.
f.	= firm.	obliquegr.	= oblique grip.
fling.	= flinging.	outw.	= outward.
forw.	= forward.	overgr.	= overgrip.
pl.	= place or placing.	swg.	= swing or swinging.
pos.	= position.	Tr.	= Trunk.
r.	= raise or raising.	turn.	= turning.
sidew.	= sideways.	upw.	= upward.
sit.	= sitting.	undergr.	= under grip.
Sp. b.	= Span bending.	V.	= Vaulting.
str.	= stretch or stretching.		

GROUP C.—ARM EXERCISES.

136. The following are the objects and effects of the simple and comparatively easy movements of the arms which are included in this group of exercises.

They provide starting positions for various trunk exercises. They develop the mobility of the shoulder blades and joints of the arm. They improve the carriage of the upper part of the trunk and at the same time they strengthen the arms for harder work.

The Arm exercises are sub-divided as follows :—

      1. Hips firm, Neck rest, etc.
      2. Arm stretchings.
      3. Arm raisings.
      4. Arm swingings.
      5. Arms flinging.

These sub-groups are employed in the following manner in the daily lesson (*i.e.* in a Table of exercises),—*Arm stretchings* and *Arm swingings*, being of an energetic nature, are used principally as "*Introductory exercises*" on account of their stimulating effect on the circulation and respiration, while the *Arm raisings* and *Arms flinging* are used as more moderate movements in the "*Final exercises.*"

The Arm exercises are also used in conjunction with other exercises to increase the effect of the latter.

Starting Position.	Exercise.	Executive Word.	Detail.
137.	**Hips—Firm** .... (Figs. 24, 25 and 26.)	" *Firm* "	Raise the hands quickly and grasp the waist firmly just above the hips, fingers together in front and thumbs behind, palms pressed well down, shoulders kept in the same position as at Attention
	Hands—Down	" *Down* "	Lower the arms sharply to the sides the shortest way

Common Faults.	Remarks.

137.

(i) Hands carried wide of the body during the movement. (ii) Heel of the hand away from the side. (iii) Hands too far back. (iv) Elbows pressed back. (v) Shoulders raised

Used as a starting position for a large number of exercises.

Besides being convenient for the purpose of getting the arms out of the way of the legs, &c., in performing certain Trunk and Leg exercises, the position of Hips firm has the advantage of transferring the weight of the arms from the shoulders and upper part of the trunk to the hips, this giving rather more freedom to the chest walls. In addition, it has the effect of bracing the whole trunk for the various exercises with which it is employed.

Incorrect.
Fig. 24.

(i) Hands not carried close to the sides. (ii) Backs of hands turned forward.

Correct.
Fig. 25.

Correct.
Fig. 26.

A. ex.

Starting Position.	Exercise.	Executive Word.	Detail.
133.	Neck—Rest .... (Fig. 27.)	" *Rest* "	Raise the hands quickly the shortest way and place them behind the upper part of the neck, finger tips just meeting, chest well raised, head erect and elbows pressed well back
	Hands—Down	" *Down* "	Lower the arms sharply to the sides the shortest way
139.	Arms—Bend .... (Fig. 28.)	" *Bend* "	Moving the elbows as little as possible from the sides, bend the arms quickly and energetically by carrying the hands the shortest way close up in front of the body till the forearms are fully bent on the upper arms, fists clenched and carried backward into line with the shoulders, the position of which should be maintained as at Attention, backs of the hands turned outward
	(Arms) downward— Stretch Note.—**Hips firm, Neck rest** and **Arms bend** may be taken from any position of the arms.	" *Stretch* "	Stretch the arms sharply downward to the sides

Common Faults.	Remarks.	

138.
(i) Head pushed forward. (ii) Elbows not pressed back enough

Used as a starting position for many exercises.
Owing to the difficulty of maintaining the position correctly it should not to be used too early.

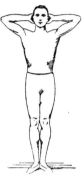

Fig. 27.

139.
(i) Hands raised sideways in bending the forearms. (ii) Elbows forced backwards and points of the shoulders forward. (iii) Elbows too far from the body and not kept down. (iv) Head poked forward. (v) Small of the back hollowed. (vi) Finger nails turned forward

Used as the starting position for all Arm stretchings and many other exercises. As it is therefore used very frequently its correct performance is of the utmost importance. Care should be taken that the breathing is in no way restricted by forcing the elbows too close to the sides.

Fig. 28.

Starting Position.	Exercise.	Executive Word.	Detail.
140. A. b.	**Arms sideways—Stretch** (Fig. 29.)	" *Stretch* "	Stretch the arms sharply sideways in line with the shoulders, palms of the hand downward, fingers closed and fully extended
141. A. b.	**Arms stretching sideways**	" *One* " .... " *Two* " *or* "*Commence*"	A. sidew. str. .... A. b.
142. A. b.	**Arms upward—Stretch** (Figs. 30, 31 & 32.)	" *Stretch* "	Stretch the arms sharply upward to their fullest extent, hands the width of the shoulders apart, palms inward, fingers closed and fully extended
143. A. b.	**Arms stretching upward**	" *One* " .... " *Two* " *or* "*Commence*"	A. upw. str. .... A. b.

Common Faults.	Remarks.
140. (i) Hands not carried the shortest way. (ii) Hands lowered or not carried sufficiently back. (iii) Shoulders raised. (iv) Back hollowed	In addition to its use as an Arm exercise the position is often taken as a starting position for other exercises.

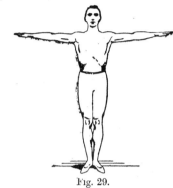

Fig. 29.

141.
As above

142.
(i) Hands not in line with the arms. (ii) Palms not fully turned inward. (iii) Fingers not fully stretched. (iv) Arms not fully stretched. (v) Arms not far enough back. (vi) Head poked forward and back hollowed.

Owing to the attachment of the pectoral muscles to the humerus the ribs are raised considerably in the performance of this exercise.

Also used as a starting position for many exercises so as to increase their effect.

The correct taking of this position under all circumstances is a useful guide as to proficiency and progress.

143.
As above

Correct.
Fig. 30.

Incorrect.
Fig. 31.

Correct.
Fig. 32.

Starting Position.	Exercise.	Executive Word.	Detail.
144. A. b.	**Arms forward—Stretch** (Fig. 33.)	" *Stretch* "	Stretch the arms sharply forward in line with the shoulders, palms of the hands inward, fingers closed and fully extended, shoulders kept well back
145. A. b.	**Arms stretching forward**	" *One* " .... " *Two* " *or* "*Commence*"	A. forw. str. .... A. b.
146. A. b.	**Left Arm upward right Arm downward — Stretch** (Fig. 34.)	" *Stretch* "	Stretch the arms sharply as directed
	(a) **Arms—Change** .... Note. — **Arms stretching sideways, upward** or **forward** may be combined as required.	" *Change* "	(a) Bend the arms and stretch them in opposite directions
147.	**Arms sideways—Raise**	" *Raise* "	Raise the arms steadily sideways in line with the shoulders, palms of the hands downward, fingers closed and fully extended
	(Arms) downward— Lower	" *Lower* "	Lower the arms steadily to the sides
148.	**Arms raising sideways**	" *One* " .... " *Two* " *or* "*Commence*"	A. sidew. r. .... A. downw. lower.

Common Faults.	Remarks.	
144. (i) Allowing the shoulders to go forward. (ii) Rounding the back	This exercise is difficult to perform correctly, and should not, therefore, be employed too early.	 Fig. 33.
145. As above		
146. (i) Trunk not kept upright. (ii) Head bent towards upward arm As above	Used as a starting position for some Lateral exercises.	
147. (i) Shoulders raised. (ii) Hands not carried sufficiently back	*Vide* para. **295** with regard to the employment of *Arms raising* as Corrective exercises.	Fig. 34.
148. As above		

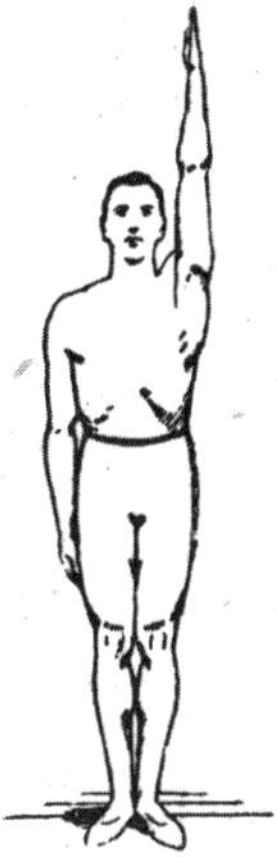

Starting Position.	Exercise.	Executive Word.	Detail.
149.	**Arms raising sideways and upward**	" *One* " .... " *Two* "	A. sidew. r. .... Turn the palms of the hands upward and immediately raise the arms to the A. upw. str. pos.
		" *Three* "	Lower the arms sideways to the level of the shoulders, keeping them well back and the palms of the hands turned upward.
		" *Four* " or "*Commence* "	Turn the palms downward and immediately lower the arms to the sides
150.	**Arms sideways and up-ward—Raise**	" *Raise* "	By a continuous movement raise the arms sideways and upward as described above, turning the hands steadily while the arms are passing the level of the shoulders
	(Arms sideways and downward)—Lower	" *Lower* " or "*Commence* "	Lower the arms to the sides by reversing the above movement
151.	**Arms raising forward upward sideways and downward**	" *One* "	Keeping the arms the width of the shoulders apart, raise them forward and continue the movement to the A. upw. str. pos.
		" *Two* " or "*Commence* "	Lower the arms sideways and downward
152.	**Arms swinging upward**	" *One* "	Swing the arms quickly, keeping them well stretched, forward and upward to the A. upw. str. pos.
	(Arms swinging down-ward)	" *Two* "	Swing the arms quickly forward and downward to the sides

Common Faults.	Remarks.
149. (i) Arms not kept far enough back during the movements	
150. As above	
151. (i) The full A. upw. str. pos. not taken before the arms are lowered when performed judging the time	
152. (i) Trunk thrown backward. (ii) Arms bent during the swing	Has a very strong stretching effect on the pectoral muscles.

Starting Position.	Exercise.	Executive Word.	Detail.
153. A. u p w. str.	**Arms swinging downward and backward** (Fig. 35.)	" *One* " .... " *Two* "	As A. swg. downw, but continued backward as far as possible Swing the arms to the A. upw. str. pos.
154. A. sidew.r.	**Arms forward—Bend** .... (Figs. 36 and 37.)	" *Bend* "	Without moving the upper arms and keeping the elbows well back, bend the forearms sharply forward and inward as much as possible
A. forw. b.	**Arms downward—Stretch**	" *Stretch* "	Stretch the arms sharply downward to the sides
155. A. forw. b.	**Arms Flinging** .... (Fig. 37.)	" *Fling* " .... *or* " *Commence* "	Without allowing the elbows to come forward, fling the arms vigorously sideways and backward to their fullest extent, keeping the palms of the hands downward, and immediately return to the position of A. forw. b. Perform the A. fling. movement until ordered to stop, observing short pauses in the forw. pos.

Common Faults.	Remarks.
153. (i) Shoulders and trunk allowed to go forward	 Fig. 35.
154. (i) Allowing the elbows to move forward and the hands to come too close together. (ii) Back too much hollowed	Used as the starting position for Arms flinging.  Fig. 36.
155. (i) Head poked forward. (ii) Flinging, not horizontal. (iii) Hands brought too close together in the recovery	Has a strong stretching effect on the pectoral muscles. 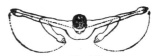 Fig. 37.

GROUP H.—ABDOMINAL EXERCISES.

217. The abdominal muscles, especially the large muscle in front of the abdomen (rectus abdominis), are those which are principally affected by the exercises of this group. These muscles play an important part in maintaining the proper carriage of the body.

The *Trunk bendings backward* stretch the front abdominal muscles, *On the Hands*, gives static contraction of the same muscles at their middle length, and the *Leg raisings* and *Knee raisings* in the lying and hanging positions shorten them. A normal length and strength of these muscles is thereby produced and the carriage consequently corrected.

Trunk bending backward also increases the mobility of the dorsal portion of the spine and thus tends to lessen the dorsal curve.

Well developed abdominal muscles provide a firm support for the organs of digestion contained in the abdomen.

Owing to the attachment of the front abdominal muscles to the pelvis and the lower part of the thorax, there is a tendency in performing these exercises to draw the ribs downwards, the effect of this being to somewhat restrict the breathing. The movements should therefore be of short duration and it may also be necessary for the instructor to remind the men to breathe freely during these exercises in order that the best results may be obtained.

The following are the sub-groups of the Abdominal exercises :—

1. Trunk bending backward.
2. Exercises " On the Hands," on ground, bench or beam.
3. Leg and Knee raising.

Abd. ex.

Starting Position.	Exercise.	Executive Word.	Detail.
218. F. sidew. pl., or F astr., or Hl. together, or F. forw. pl., and H. f , or A. b., or A. upw. str.	....	" *One* "	Keeping the knees straight, bend the upper part of the trunk slowly backward, the head commencing the movement and kept well back with the chin drawn in. The bending should *not* be made from the waist alone, but the whole spine should be arched.
		" *Two* " or	By reversing the movement raise the trunk to the starting pos.
	(Trunk backward—bend)	" *Bend* "	
	(Upward—Stretch) .... *Note. — Trunk bending backward* may also be taken with *Foot support* on wall bars or bench, and to make the exercise still stronger the knee of the standing leg may be bent at the same time as the body.	" *Stretch* "	
219. 1 pace from and facing wall bars	**On the third (fourth, fifth) bar, left Foot—Support**	"*Support*"	Keeping the knee straight, raise the left leg and insert the foot between the third and fourth bars, gripping them firmly by pressing the toes against the latter and the heel against the former.
	Foot inward—Place	" *Place* "	Resume the starting pos.
219A. 1 pace from and facing the wall bars. F. support, H. f., or A. b., or A. upw. str.	**Trunk bending backward** **Trunk backward—Bend** **Upward—Stretch**	" *One* " " *Two* " " *Bend* " "*Stretch*"	As in para. 218.

Common Faults.	Remarks.

218.
(i) The bending made only in the small of the back. (ii) Head not carried back sufficiently. (iii) Chin not drawn in. (iv) Knees bent. (v) Breathing restricted.

As one of the objects of this exercise is to stretch the dorsal portion of the spine a very great bending backward is not required. At the commencement of the movement the body should however be stretched well upward and then the bending backward in the dorsal region commenced. At first, the bending should be only slight but correct, and as progress is made the bending may be increased by degrees.

Progression in the *Trunk bendings backward* is obtained, as in the Lateral exercises, by raising the centre of gravity from H. f., to A. b., to A. upw. str. ; the position of N. r. is not as a rule used with these exercises owing to the difficulty experienced in maintaining the position correctly, a faulty N. r. position being very likely to counteract some of the otherwise good effects of the exercises of this group.

Fig. 74.

Correct.   Fig. 75.

219.

Used as a starting position for *Trunk bending backward.*

Incorrect.   Fig. 76.

Starting Position.	Exercise.	Executive Word.	Detail.
219B. 1 short pace from and facing the wall bars.	**On the third (fourth, fifth) bar, left Foot—Support**	*"Support"*	Keeping the right knee straight, raise the left leg, and insert the foot between the third and fourth bars, gripping them firmly by pressing the toes against the latter and the heel against the former. In this case the left knee should be bent.
	Foot inward—Place	*" Place "*	Resume the starting position.
219c. F. full o., F. support, H. f., or A. b., or A. upw. str.	**Trunk bending backward**	*" One "*	Keeping the head, trunk and right leg in the same relative position to each other, *incline* the body backward by straightening the left knee.
		" Two "....	By reversing the movement resume the starting position.
	(Trunk backward—Bend)	*" Bend "*	
	(Upward—Stretch)	*" Stretch "*	
220. Facing bench	**Sitting on bench—Down**	*" Down "*	Turning quickly about (moving "free") sit on the bench, heels on ground, toes pointed, legs straight, body and head erect, arms straight, wrists resting on front edge of bench, palms inward.
	On the Feet—Up	*" Up "*	Spring to attention, turning about ("free") so as to face the bench.
	Sitting on ground—Down	*" Down "*	Passing through the full K. b. pos. place both hands on the ground a little to the rear and at the same time shoot the legs to the front, toes pointed, legs straight, body and head erect, palms of the hands on the ground.
	On the Feet—Up	*" Up "*	Pressing sharply from the ground with the hands and drawing the feet in, spring to Attention.

Common Faults.	Remarks.
219B. Standing leg not directly under the trunk (*i.e.*, not perpendicular).	The correct bar to take is the one which ensures the thigh of the supported leg being horizontal, while the erect position of the rest of the body is maintained.
220.	
	" Sitting " on bench and on ground are used, with *Foot support,* as starting positions for *Trunk bending backward.*
	Foot support may be taken at the wall bars with both feet inserted between two of the bars at the required height, or with living support as described under " Class Arrangements " (*vide* para. **108**).

Starting Position	Exercise.	Executive Word.	Detail.
221. Sit., F. support and H. f., or A. b., or A. upw. str.	**Trunk backward— Bend**	" *Bend* "	Keeping the body erect and well braced up, incline it steadily backward as far as required.
	Upward—Stretch .... (Fig. 77.)	" *Stretch* "	
222.	**On the Hands** .... (Fig. 78.)	" *One* "	Bend the knees quickly outward, incline the trunk slightly forward and place the palms of the hands on the ground rather more than the width of the shoulders apart, fingers turned slightly inward, arms straight and nearly vertical. The back should be kept straight and the head in the same relative position to the shoulders as at Attention.
		" *Two* "....	Keeping the arms straight shoot the feet backward till the body and legs are straight and fully stretched, the weight supported by the toes and hands. Heels together, feet at the normal foot-angle, arms at right angles to the body, head in the
		or " *Down* "	same relative position as at Attention.

Common Faults.	Remarks.
221. (i) Back rounded. (ii) Head poked forward. (iii) Breathing restricted.	It should be noted that the "Trunk bending" is really a "Trunk falling"; i.e., no movement takes place in the upper part of the trunk, the erect position of it being maintained throughout the exercise. Progression, besides being obtained by the starting position of the arms, can also be made as follows, viz., by stopping the backward inclination at 45°, then with the body in line with the legs and later continuing the inclination downward as far as possible.

Fig. 77.

222. (i) Rounding the back and dropping the head forward in the first movement. (ii) Body dropped slackly between the arms. (iii) Slackening the abdominal muscles and thereby hollowing the back. (iv) Raising the seat. (v) Head not kept in its relative position to the body.	The exercise is here described for both hands and feet on the ground, but progression is best obtained by first taking it with the hands higher than the feet (on bench or beam), then with hands and feet on the ground, and afterwards with the feet higher than the hands (on bench, &c.). When the hands are on a bench or beam the positions are taken in a similar manner, except that the thumbs are placed against the near edge of the bench or beam. When the feet are to be on a bench, &c., the position is taken in three movements, the first as described, the second placing left foot on bench and the third placing right foot on bench.

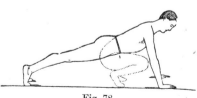

Fig. 78.

Starting Position.	Exercise.	Executive Word.	Detail.
	(Hands inward — Turn)	" *Turn* "	Turn the left and then the right hand inward.
	(Hands forward — Turn)	" *Turn* "	Turn the hands as described.
	On the Feet	" *One* "	Resume quickly the first position of *On the Hands.*
		" *Two* " or " *Up* "	Spring to Attention.
223. On the Hands or ditto with Hands inward turn	**Arms—Bend**	" *Bend* "	Without in any other way altering the position of the body lower it close to the ground by bending the arms.
	(Arms)—Stretch	" *Stretch* "	Resume the starting position by straightening the arms.
224. On the Hands	**Left Leg—Raise** (Fig. 79.)	" *Raise* "	Keeping the leg straight raise it as high as possible, toe pointed, without altering the position of the body.
		" *Lower* "	Lower the leg to the starting pos.
225. On the Hands	**Left Arm forward and upward—Raise** (Fig. 80.)	" *Raise* "	Raise the left arm steadily as ordered without altering the position of the body more than is absolutely necessary.
		" *Lower* "	Lower the arm to the starting pos.

Common Faults.	Remarks.
223. (i) Altering the straight position of the body.	The bending of the arms increases the effect on the abdominal muscles.
224.	This exercise has also a lateral and an oblique effect on the abdominal muscles.

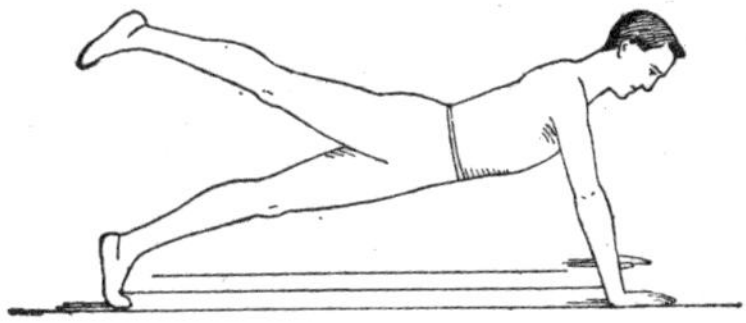

Fig. 79.

225.	Has also a lateral and oblique effect on the abdominal muscles.

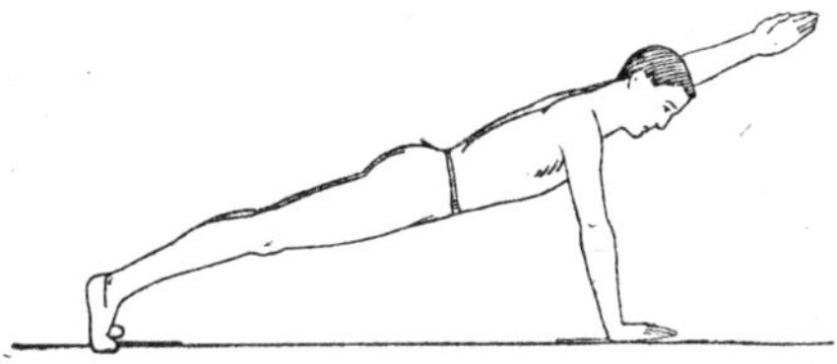

Fig. 80.

Starting Position.	Exercise.	Executive Word.	Detail.
226. In front of wall bars	**On the top bar—Up** .... **On the Feet—Down**	" *Up* " " *Down* "	Described under " Jumping and Vaulting." exercises (*vide* para. 278)
227. Overg. (wall bar or beam)	**Left Knee—Raise**	" *Raise* "	Bend the left knee and raise it upward until the thigh is at right angles to the body and the lower leg hanging straight downward with the toe pointing to the ground.
	(Knee)—Lower	" *Lower* "	Lower the leg to its original position.
228. Overgr., K. r.	**Leg Forward—Stretch**	" *Stretch* "	Keeping the thigh raised, stretch the leg and foot forward in line with it.
	(Knee)—Bend	" *Bend* "	Bend the knee to K. r. pos.
229. Overgr. (wall bar or beam)	**Knees—Raise** .... (Fig. 81.) **(Knees)—Lower**	" *Raise* " " *Lower* "	Raise both knees as described above. Lower both knees.
230. Overgr., Ks. r.	**Left Leg (Legs) forward—Stretch** (Fig. 81.) **(Knees)—Bend**	" *Stretch* " " *Bend* "	Stretch one or both legs as described above. Bend one or both knees.
231. Overgr. (wall bar or beam)	**Legs raising**	" *One* "	Keeping the knees straight and toes pointed raise the legs to a horizontal position.
		" *Two* "	Lower the legs to their original position.

Common Faults.	Remarks.
226.	Used as a starting position for *Knee* and *Leg Raising*.
227. (i) Lower leg not vertical. (ii) Breathing restricted. (iii) Head not kept back.	
228. (i) Breathing restricted. (ii) Head not kept back.	
229. As above.	The knees may occasionally be raised as high as possible, on the word, *Full knees raise.* 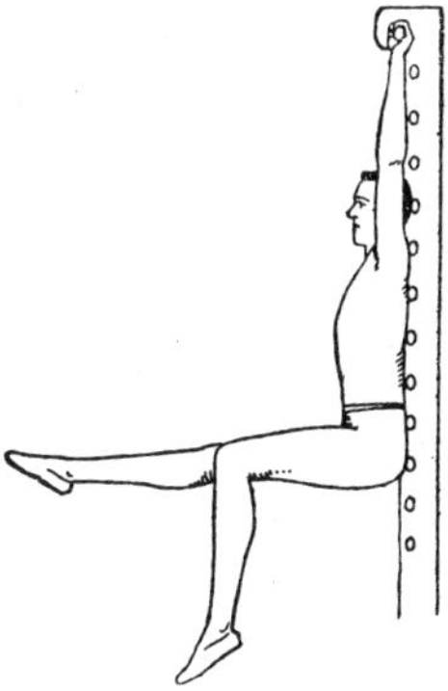
230. As above.	
231. (i) Breathing restricted. (ii) Head not kept back.	The legs may occasionally be raised as high as possible (*Full legs raising*).

Fig. 81.

Starting Position.	Exercise.	Executive Word.	Detail.
232.			
	Lying on the back— Down	" *Down* "	Passing through the full K. b. pos. place both hands on the ground a little to the rear, and at the same time lower the body quickly backward to the ground and shoot the legs to the front. The body should thus be stretched flat on the back, feet together, toes pointed, arms to the sides, palms of the hands on the ground.
	On the Feet—Up	" *Up* "	Pressing sharply on the ground with the elbows and hands and drawing the feet in, spring smartly to Attention. If the command is given when lying in the A. upw. str. pos., the arms should be swung forward and downward to the ground in executing this movement.
233. Lying, A. upw. r., or N. r.	**Left Leg raise** .... (Fig. 82.) **Legs raising.**	" *One* "	Keeping the knees straight and the toes pointed raise the leg or legs steadily to an angle of 45°, without raising the seat from the ground.
		" *Two* "	Lower the leg or legs steadily to the ground.

Common Faults.	Remarks.
232.	Used as a starting position for *Legs raising*.
233. (i) Breathing restricted. (ii) Knees bent. (iii) Back hollowed.	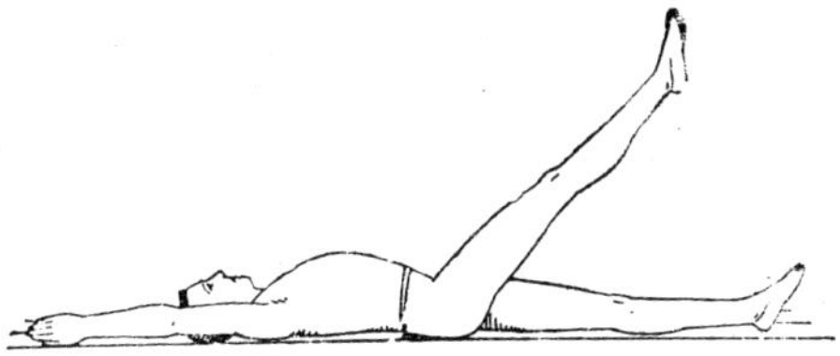

Fig. 82.

3

Special & Supplementary Tables for Physical Training, 1914-17

The speed at which the German Army advanced through Belgium and France meant that it was crucial for the British Army to train as many soldiers as possible in the shortest amount of time. The lack of equipment and insufficient number of gymnasia meant that most of the training had to take place out in camps. While the physical training tables used for recruits were designed to be spread over 110 hours, physical training for the new armies would have to be completed in under half that time. Training programmes had to be shortened, simplified and, with the aid of diagrams, be able to be taught by any intelligent NCO without access to physical training equipment.[1] These revised exercise training tables, although simplified, were compiled with the same scientific knowledge that was utilised by the 1908 tables and *Manual of Physical Training*. The supplementary training tables printed in 1915 (which were subsequently updated and reprinted in 1916 and 1917) included additional training tables for trained soldiers and specific exercises for bombers, officer cadets and soldiers in trenches, as well as physical training exercises to be carried out in the morning and remedial tables. Supplementary tables that were printed after 1917 would include a 'Games' chapter, which was initially a standalone manual printed in 1916 for use by physical training instructors with physical training tables.

The course carried out at Aldershot in September 1914 to produce a new batch of physical training instructors had to be significantly adjusted to suit the circumstances. The pre-war course, which would normally last four months, would now take place over twenty-one days and would provide the NCO with the sufficient grounding for them to be assistant instructors in their units while remaining under the supervision of an Army Gymnastic Staff instructor.[2]

Duration of Course: 21 Working Days.
Example of Time-Table for a Week

	Morning.
9–10 a.m.	Physical Training Table under Staff Instructors.
10.15–10.45 a.m.	Bayonet instruction under ditto.
10.45–11.15 a.m.	Physical Training 'communicating drill'.
11.30 –12 noon.	Bayonet instruction.
12 noon – 12.30 p. m.	Class-taking and instruction in Physical Training games.
	Afternoon.
2.15–3.10 p. m.	P.T. Table under staff instruction.*
3.20–3.50 p. m.	Bayonet instruction.
3.50–4.15 p. m.	Class taking and lectures by Staff Instructors.

*From second week onwards, massed table of Physical Training from 2.15 to 2.45 p. m. followed by games for fifteen minutes.

On Saturdays the working hours are from 9 a.m. to 12 noon.

Voluntary hours during the week under supervision of Staff Instructors: 5.30 to 7.30 p.m. These are attended by the vast majority of N.C.Os. under instruction.

Examination.
Each class is examined n Bayonet Training Lessons and trench work during the course. Individual examination in practical work and powers of instruction at the end of course. Each individual is examined in Physical Training on last day of course and his qualities as an Instructor assessed.[3]

40
———
W.O.
———
2936

SUPPLEMENTARY PHYSICAL TRAINING TABLES.

1916.

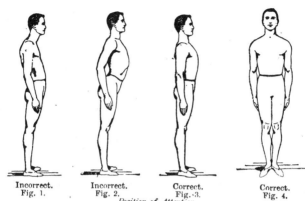

| Incorrect.
Fig. 1. | Incorrect.
Fig. 2. | Correct.
Fig. 3. | Correct.
Fig. 4. |

Position of Attention.

Fig. 1. Faults :—Head poked forward, chest and lumbar region of back hollowed, abdomen pushed forward.

Fig. 2. Faults :—Shoulders unduly drawn back, chest forced out, back hollowed, weight on fore part of feet ; position strained and unnatural.

Figs. 3 & 4 Correct, erect position, without strain.

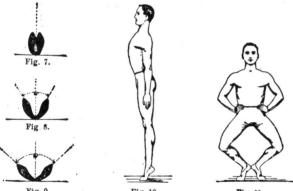

Fig. 7.

Fig. 8.

Fig. 9.

Position of Feet.

Fig. 7. "Feet—close" (F. cl.).
Fig. 8. "Feet—open" (F. o.).
Fig. 9. "Feet full open" (F. full o.).

Fig. 10.
"Heels—raise" (Hl. r.).
Heels together and lifted as high as possible, body erect—as at "attention."

Fig. 11.
"Knees—bend" (K. b.)
Heels kept together, body not inclined forward.

(B 5842)

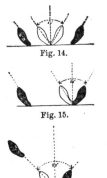

Fig. 14.

Fig. 15.

Fig. 17.
Position of Feet.
Fig. 14. "Feet astride—place."
Fig. 15. "Left Foot sideways—place."
Fig. 17. "Left Foot outward—place."

Fig. 19.
Position of Outward Lunge.
Body allowed to drop forward without jerking, head and trunk maintaining their relative positions.

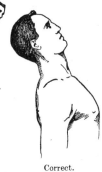

Correct.
Fig. 22.
"Head backward—bend." Chin kept down, breathing unrestrained, movement not extended to back.

Incorrect.
Fig. 21.
Faults:—Chin forced upward, shoulders raised, back hollowed, breathing restricted.

Incorrect.
Fig. 24.

Correct.
Fig. 25.

Correct.
Fig. 26.

Position of "Hips—firm."
Fig. 24. Faults:—Head poked forward, shoulders forced back, hands not grasping hips, back hollowed.
Figs. 25 & 26.—Position of shoulders as at "attention" maintained, heel of hand forced down, fingers inclined slightly upwards, hip grasped firmly.

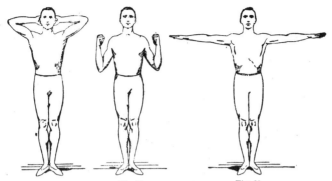

Fig. 27.　　　　　Fig. 28.
Fig. 28. *Position of "Arms—bend."* (A. b.).
Correct :—Finger nails pointing inward, forearms vertical, elbows kept away from sides and in line with centre of trunk.

Fig. 29
Position of " Arms sideways—stretch."
Keep the hands level with the shoulders throughout, extending them as far apart as possible by forcing them outwards from the shoulders.

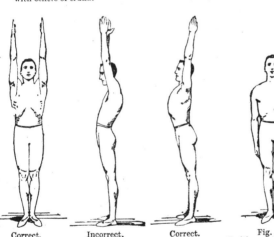

Correct.　　　Incorrect.　　　Correct.
Fig. 30.　　　Fig. 31.　　　Fig. 32.
Position of " Arms upward—stretch " (A. upw. str.).
By exerting considerable tension force the hands as high as possible, keeping them the width of the shoulders apart with palms turned inward. It is important that the erect position of attention is maintained by the rest of the body.

Fig. 34.
Position of " Left Arm upward , right Arm downward — stretch"
(1 A. upw., 1 A. downw str.).

(B 5842)

A 2

Supplementary Physical Training Tables, 1915.

HINTS TO REGIMENTAL INSTRUCTORS WHEN CONDUCTING THE TRAINED SOLDIERS' TABLES.

1. Enforce strictest discipline tempered with tact, without which the training loses greatly in value.

2. Always ensure that the men are kept warm.

3. Check faults as shortly as possible and above all avoid a large amount of talking.

4. Keep the class "lively" and interested. An aid to this is the use of "Quickening Exercises," of which the following are a few of the simplest examples :—

    (a) Falling in in two ranks as quickly as possible at different spots indicated by the Instructor.

    (b) Racing to a spot a short distance away, and back.

    (c) Assuming the sitting position, and getting up again as quickly as possible.

    (d) Hopping with Leg raising sideways, etc., etc.

5. Never neglect to encourage a class for any improvement, even though it may only be slight.

6. NEVER keep men long in a position of strain.

7. Remember "Trunk backward bend"=an exaggerated " Head backward bend," with the movement only extended as far as the shoulder blades.

OBJECT AND SCOPE OF EXERCISES.

I.—TRAINED SOLDIERS' TABLE.

(i.) Strength and Endurance.

The exercises are so arranged that all the muscles of the body are scientifically worked and strengthened.

No muscles are neglected. The longer the course of these exercises is continued the greater will be the power added to those muscles required for MARCHING DIGGING, RAPID FIRING and BAYONET FIGHTING, and with the strengthening of these muscles comes greater endurance.

(ii.) Health.

All the internal organs of the body—the heart, lungs, liver, kidneys and the digestive organs—are worked and stimulated : by this means health is improved and vigour increased.

(iii.) Nerve.

There are no mechanical, or purely muscle forcing, exercises in the Table. Each exercise is one of co-ordination—movements actuated and controlled by the brain. The nerve is the connecting link between brain and muscle, and every time it is brought into use by the brain to work a muscle it is toned and strengthened.

(B 5842)   A 3

(iv.) Executive Action.	By continually performing exercises of co-ordination, brain and muscle are brought into sympathy with one another and EXECUTIVE ACTION — quickness of action, presence of mind—is developed.
(v.) Brain and Will-power.	The necessity of always having to use the brain in the performance of the exercises and, in some, to isolate groups of muscle against natural inclination, develops Will-power.
(vi.) Foundation of all Trainings.	To sum up, Physical Training should be regarded as the foundation of all training, for the benefits derived from it are :—

a. Strengthening of the Body = Power to overcome obstacles and perform arduous duties.

b. Improvement and maintenance of Health = Endurance of hardships and privations.

c. Quickening of the Brain = More rapid assimilation of instruction in other trainings, orders readily understood and rapidly executed.

d. Increase of Power of Mental Concentration = The foundation of good shooting.

(vii.) Durstion of Table, etc.	Time required to complete the Table is about half an hour. It should be performed daily six days a week.

(viii.) **Instructors.** All Officers and N.C.Os. should be taught to put their men through these exercises, but Recruits' Tables should only be carried out by Instructors in possession of an Aldershot Physical Training Certificate.

2. MORNING TABLES.

The exercises in the Morning Tables are arranged on the same scientific principles as those in the Trained Soldiers' Tables, but are of a milder degree. The short time in which they can be performed make them most convenient for those who wish to "keep fit," but who, owing to arduous office work, are prevented from devoting more time to exercise. They can be performed two or three times a day as opportunity offers.

3. REMEDIAL TABLE.

Constipation and slight stomach troubles can be benefited by performing this Table of Exercises. They are not severe, but should there be any question of ulcers or diarrhœa they should not be performed.

The breathing should be always easy and natural during the exercises.

1. TRAINED SOLDIERS' TABLE—I.

N.B.—This table is intended for "trained" soldiers who have not recently done any Physical Training, or for those whose previous Recruits' Physical Training was incomplete.

A.—INTRODUCTORY EXERCISES.

1. L. Ex.   A. b., Hl. r., K.b.—**Arms stretching sideways** (4 times).   Exercise to be performed twice.

2. N. Ex.   **Head bending backward** (3 times).

3. A. Ex.   A. b.—**Arms stretching sideways, upward, and forward** (3 times, varying sequence of direction).

4. Tr. Ex.   A. b., F. sidew. pl.—**Trunk turning** (twice in each direction).

5. L. Ex.   H. f.—**Foot placing sideways and Heels raising** (3 times each foot).

B.—GENERAL EXERCISES.

1. Prep. for   F. astr. A. upw. str.—**Trunk bending back-**
Sp. b.   **ward** (3 times).

Comp. Ex.   F. astr., H. f.—**Trunk bending forward and full downward** (twice).

Supp. Ex.   H. f.—**Heels raising and Knees bending** (3 times).

2. Bal. Ex. (a).   H. f.—**Leg raising sideways** (3 times each leg).

   or   (b).   H. f.—**Leg raising forward** (3 times each leg).

3. Lat. Ex. (a).   A. b., F. sidew. pl.—**Trunk bending sideways quickly** (3 times each side).

   or   (b).   On the Hands—**On one Hand turn** (twice on each).

4. Adb. Ex. (a). On the Hands—**Leg raising** (twice each leg).

or (b). (ground permitting) :

Lying A. upw. r.—**Legs raising** (3 times).

5. Dor. Ex. A. b., F. sidew. pl., Tr. forw. b.—**Arms stretching sideways** (3 times).

Exercise to be performed twice.

6. Mar. Ex. Quick March
Double March } To be done each time.
Marching on the Toes

H. f.—**With Knee raising quick mark time.**
Double mark time—**With Hips firm Knees raise.**
H. f.—**On alternate Feet hop.**
Two to be done each time.

7. J. & V. **Upward jumping.**
Upward jumping with Arms raising sideways.
Upward jumping with turning.
Two to be done each time.

Forward jumping.
With three paces forward off the left (or right) Foot jump.
One to be done each time.

C.—FINAL EXERCISES.

1. L. Ex. H. f.—**Heels raise.** (4 times).
2. Corr. Ex. **Arms raising forward and upward, lowering sideways and downward** (until the action of the Heart and Lungs is eased).

TRAINED SOLDIERS' TABLE—II.

N.B.—This Table is intended for "trained" soldiers who have recently done Physical Training regularly.

A.—INTRODUCTORY EXERCISES.

1. L. Ex. H. f., F. full o.—**Heels raising and full Knees bending** (4 times).

2. N. Ex. (a.) **Head bending backward** (twice).

   or (b.) **Head turning** (twice in each direction).

3. A. Ex. A. b.—**Arms stretching forward, sideways and upward** (3 times varying sequence of direction).

4. Tr. Ex. A. b., F. sidew. pl.— **Trunk turning quickly with Arms stretching upward** (twice in each direction).

5. L. Ex. H. f., F. full o.—**Outward lunging** (3 times each Foot).

B.—GENERAL EXERCISES.

1. Prep. for F. astr. A. upw. str.—**Trunk bending back-**
   Sp. b. **ward** (3 times).

   Comp. Ex. F. astr. H. f.—**Trunk bending forward and full downward** (twice).

   Supp. Ex. H. f.—**Heels raising and Knees bending** (3 times).

2. Bal. Ex. (a). H. f.—**Leg raising forward, sideways and backward** (twice each leg).

   or (b). H. f., K. r.—**Leg stretching forward** (twice each leg).

3. Lat. Ex. (a). F. cl., 1 A. upw. 1 A. downw. str.—**Trunk bending sideways** (twice to each side).

   or (b). On one hand—**Leg raising** (twice each leg).

4. Abd. Ex. On the Hands.—**Arms bend** (3 times), and add later with **Leg raising** (twice with each Leg).

or (ground permitting) :
        Lying, **A.** upw. r.—**Legs raising.** (3 times).

5. Dor. Ex. F. astr. A. upw. str., Tr. forw. b.—**Arms swinging downward and backward** (3 times).
        Exercise to be performed twice.

6. Mar. Ex. Quick march.
           Double march.   } To be done each time.
           Marching on the Toes.

H. f.—**With Knee raising quick march.**

Double mark time—**With Hips firm Knees raise.**

Quick march—**With Hips firm on alternate Feet hop.**

        Two to be done each time.

7. J. & V. **Upward jumping with Arms swinging upward.**
Forward jumping.

With turning, 3 paces forward off the left (or right) Foot jump.

        Two to be done each time.

C.—FINAL EXERCISES.

1. L. Ex.   H. f.—**Foot placing sideways** (twice each Foot).

2. Tr. Ex.   H. f., F. cl.—**Trunk turning** (twice in each direction).

3. Corr. Ex.   **Arms raising forward and upward, lowering sideways and downward** (until the action of the Heart and Lungs is eased).

2. MORNING TABLE (5 Minutes).

Vide Manual
of P.T.
para.

149 1. Corr. Ex. **Arms raising sideways and upward** (8 times).

113 2. L. Ex. H. f.—**Heels raising and Knees bending** (4 times).

131 3. N. Ex. (a.) **Head bending backward** (3 times).

134 (b.) **Head turning** (twice in each direction).

N.B.*4. Tr. Ex. H. f., Tr. forw. b.—**Trunk rolling** (4 times to left over to right, then 4 times right over to left).

139 5. A. Ex. **Arms stretching forward, upward, sideways and downward** (3 times).
to 145

N.B.*6. Bal. Ex. H. f., K. r.—**Leg stretching backward** (3 times each Leg).

208 7. Lat. Ex. H. f., F. astr., Tr. turn.—**Trunk turning quickly** from the left to the right and vice versa (4 times).

233 8. Abd. Ex. Lying, N. r.—**Legs** raising (4 times). If weak, with bent knees.

235 9. Dor. Ex. F. astr. A. upw. str.—**Trunk bending forward and downward** (4 times making one movement of the two motions).
and
236

115 10. L. Ex. H. f., F. full o.—**Heels raising and full Knees bending** (3 times).

151 11. Corr. Ex. **Arms raising forward and upward, lowering sideways and downward** (until action of Heart and Lungs eased).

MORNING TABLE (10 Minutes).

Vide Manual
of P.T.
para.

149   1. Corr. Ex., **Arms raising sideways and upward** (8 times).

112   2. L. Ex.   H. f.—**Heels raising and Knees bending** (4 times).

131   3. N. Ex.   (a.) **Head bending backward** (3 times).

133   (b.) **Head bending sideways** (twice to each side).

139   4. A. Ex.   **Arms stretching forward, upward, sideways and downward** (3 times).

to 145

N.B.*5. Tr. Ex.   H. f., F. astr., Tr. forw. b.—**Trunk rolling** (4 times to left over to right, then 4 times to right over to left).

125   6. L. Ex.   H. f., F. full o.—**Outward lunging** (3 times in each direction).

N.B.*7. Bal. Ex.   H. f., K. r.—**Leg stretching backward** (3 times each Leg).

210   8. Lat. Ex.   A. b. F. astr.—**Trunk bending sideways** (3 times in each direction).

233   9. Abd. Ex.   Lying, N. r.—**Legs raising** (4 times).

235   10. Dor. Ex.   F. astr. A. upw. str.—**Trunk bending forward and downward** (4 times making one movement of the two motions).

and

236

223   11. Abd. Ex.   On the Hands (if weak, Hands on bed or chairs).—**Arms bending** (3 or 4 times).

---

* N.B. **Trunk rolling.**—Positions of Trunk sideways bend, Trunk backward bend, Trunk sideways bend and Trunk forward bend are taken up in rotation by a continuous rolling movement without pausing. H. f., K.r., **Leg stretching backward.**—The Knee is slowly stretched and the Leg carried back to the position of Leg backward raise, then the motion is reversed and the starting position again assumed.

207 12. Tr. Ex. H. f., F. astr., Tr. half left (and
219   right) turn.—(a.) **Trunk bending
                   backward** (twice).
235   (b.) **Trunk bending forward** (twice).
115 13. L. Ex.   H. f., F. full o.—**Heels raising and full
                   Knees bending** (3 times).
134 14. N. Ex.   **Head turning** (twice in each direction).
151 15. Corr. Ex. **Arms raising forward and upward,
                   lowering sideways and downward**
                   (until action of Heart and Lungs
                   eased).

3. PHYSICAL TRAINING.

REMEDIAL TABLE (for the treatment of Constipation, Indigestion, etc.).

115 1. L. Ex.   H. f., F. full o.—**Heels raising and full
                   Knees bending** (4 times).
219 2. Tr. Ex.   H. f., F. sidew. pl., Tr. half left (right)
(a)   turn.—**Trunk bending backward**
                   (3 times in each position).
*   3. Tr. Ex.   H. f., F. astr., Tr. forw. b.—**Trunk
                   rolling** (3 circles to left over to
                   right and 3 vice-versa).
233 4. Abd. Ex. Lying, N. r.—**Legs raising** (4 times).
208 5. Tr. Ex.   H. f., F. astr. pl., Tr. to left turn.—
                   Trunk turning quickly to right
                   (left) (3 times in each direction).
149 6. Br. Ex.   **Arms raising sideways and upward.**

* *Vide* Note, Morning Tables.

219 7. Tr. Ex.   F. astr. A. upw. str.—**Trunk bending**
235   **forward and downward, stretch-**
236   **ing forward, upward and back-**
ward (3 or 4 times, no pause
being made in the Trunk backward bend position).

8. Abd. Ex. H. f., Sit. **(Knees slightly bent, Feet fixed under some suitable obstacle).** Trunk leaning backward until it touches the floor and after a slight pause raise the body up and lean forward as far as possible (4 times).

222 9. Abd. Ex. On the Hands.—**Feet placing forward** (4 times).

252 10. Mar. Ex. H. f.—**With Knee raising quick mark time.**

113 11. L. Ex. H. f.—**Heels raising and Knees bending** (3 times).

151 12. Br. Ex. **Arms raising forward and upward, lowering sideways and downward** (until the action of the Heart and Lungs eased).

THE BATTALION DAILY PRACTICE.

Physical Training and Bayonet Fighting Practice to be done regularly.

Physical training and bayonet fighting should be practised regularly during the whole of a soldier's service at home (vide W.O. Letter 69/2679 (A.G. 2a) of 12.7.15), and to derive full and lasting benefit every man should do one hour a day, five days in the week.

Whole Battalion exercised in one hour.

If properly organised, the whole battalion (except recruits) can perform their physical training and bayonet fighting daily practice in a single hour providing the officers and non-commissioned officers have all been trained by a series'of 6-day regimental courses.

Regimental Courses.

Selected assistant instructors are given classes of approximately four officers and twelve non-commissioned officers who are struck off all other duties two hours a day for six consecutive days, to be taught (a) to put the trained soldiers through their P.T. table, and (b) to instruct in the bayonet fighting daily practice, one hour being devoted to each. During the first half-hour the instructor will impart practical instruction, and for the remaining half-hour class-taking will be practised, the members of the class first working in pairs and later with increasingly larger squads.

Courses to be continuous.

The courses should always be continuous so that commencing on a Monday they will finish on a Saturday.

The hours selected must be other than the battalion physical training and bayonet fighting hour when all qualified officers and non-commissioned officers are required to supervise and assist.

Arrangements for the Battalion hour.

During the hour in which the whole battalion performs its training, one half should commence with physical training while the other half does bayonet fighting, and at the end of the first half-hour change about. Similarly to avoid congestion at the final assault practice course, which should be extended to accommodate as many as possible, some squads should start with the final assault, and do their direction and strengthening practices later.

Advantages of an organised system.

The chief advantages of organising the battalion physical training and bayonet fighting on the above lines are : —

(1) The duration of the training of the whole battalion being only one hour, it can be easily fitted in with other trainings.

(2) Young officers and non-commissioned officers are given opportunities for taking squads, rapidly learn to give words of command and gain confidence in themselves.

(3) The squads under instruction being small, the individual can be studied and given proper attention.

(4) The training being organised for small squads, it can be continued on wet days in barracks, &c., and as a means to keeping fit and efficient whenever opportunites offer overseas.

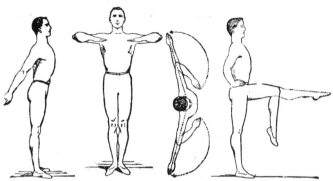

Fig. 35.   Fig. 36.   Fig. 37.

Fig. 35. *Final position of " Arms swinging downward*
and backward."

Figs. 36 and 37.   *Position of " Arms forward—bend "*
(A. forw. b.) and " Arms—fling."

Elbows kept well back, hands move horizontally and
the backward movement not forcibly checked,
position of head and trunk to remain unaltered.

Fig. 60.
Position of " Left Knee—
raise " (Left K. r.) and
from it " Leg forward—
stretch " (L. forw. str.).

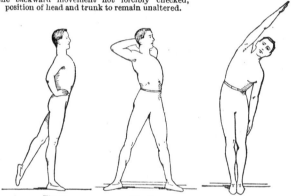

Fig. 61.   Fig. 66.   Fig. 67.

Fig. 61. *Position of " Left Leg backward—raise "* (Left L. backw. r.).

Fig. 66. " Trunk to the left—turn" (with " Neck—rest "). In all Trunk turning
hips kept to the front, upper part of trunk (*i.e.*, above the waist) turned as
far as possible in direction named, the relative positions of head and arms
being maintained.

Fig. 67. *Position of " Trunk to the left—bend "* (Tr. sidew. b.), from " Feet—close,"
" Right Arm upward, left Arm downward—stretch." Trunk not inclined
forward or backward, relative position of head maintained.

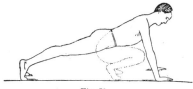

Fig. 78.

Position of " On the Hands ."

Fingers slightly inward, hands rather wider apart than the shoulders, arms straight and nearly vertical, toes apart and body straight as at " attention."

Fig. 74.
Position of " Trunk backward—bend." An exaggerated " Head backward—bend " by extending the movement down the spine as low as the bottom of the shoulder blades without hollowing the lumbar region of the back.

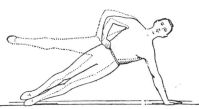

Fig. 71.

Position of " On the left Hand—turn," " Leg—raise."

The leg is raised as high as possible and the hip is allowed to *follow* the movement.

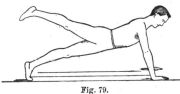

Fig. 79.

Position of " On the Hands ; Leg—raise."

Keeping the leg straight raise it as high as possible, toe pointed, without altering position of body.

Fig. 82.
Position of " Right Leg—raise " from " Lying, Arms upward — raise." With toes pointed, leg raised to an angle of 45°, keeping knees and back straight.

81

Correct.
Fig. 83.   Fig. 84.   Incorrect.
Fig. 85.

"Trunk forward—bend" (Tr. forw. b.).
Fig. 83. With "Hips—firm." Correct.
Fig. 84. With "Arms upward—stretch."
Fig. 85. Faults :—Back rounded, arms allowed to drop forward.

Fig. 86.   Fig. 92.   Fig. 93.

Fig. 86. From " Trunk forward—bend" (Tr. forw. b.) "Trunk downward—bend"
(Tr. downw. b.). Correct position :—Back kept straight as possible.
Fig. 92. "Double—march." Inclining body slightly forward, double on toes with
easy springy strides, maintaining correct carriage. Arms slightly bent (135°)
and swinging easily from shoulders. Fists clenched, backs of hands outward.
Fig. 93. " Upward—jump," Raise the heels, bend the knees, keeping the body
erect and spring vertically upward, fully extending body and legs and carrying
head and feet backward without bending the knees. Land lightly by coming
to the "full knees bend" position, thus neutralising the shock.

(B 5842) Wt. w. 18495—5775 100M 3/16 H & S P 16/153 T.S. 1209.

4

Bayonet Training, 1916-18

In early 1915, the Army Gymnastic Staff (AGS) became responsible for training troops in bayonet fighting, bringing the training methods in line with what soldiers could expect in battle. The AGS were renamed as the Physical & Bayonet Training Staff; a title which would remain until 1918, when the responsibility for bayonet training was transferred to the control of the Musketry Staff. The transition would be slow and all member of the Musketry Staff would have to complete the physical training course at Aldershot.[1]

The methods of bayonet fighting of 1914 were continually developed until the Headquarters Gymnasium in Aldershot produced a new manual for bayonet fighting, which would be distributed widely to the British Army in 1916 and subsequently reprinted in 1918. The equipment required for these new techniques was at first not readily available in sufficient quantities. Long sticks were used against sacks containing straw, suspended from rudimentary scaffolding to represent the enemy, as substitutes for the pre-1914 spring-loaded bayonets and heavily padded jackets.[2]

In 1916, Major R. B. Campbell, a Gordon Highlander attached to the AGS, arrived in France with the intention of establishing physical training in the French theatre of war. The success of the physical and bayonet training in Aldershot led to Campbell presenting the course in France to generals Allenby, Haig and French. They were impressed with what they saw and ordered for it to be deployed in France. During peacetime this course had run for four months at Aldershot, but on the battlefields of France time did not allow commanders to think in weeks, let alone months. The course was reduced to six days and covered the basics of bayonet and physical training instruction.[3]

In 1917, the success of the AGS bayonet training in the UK and France led to instructors being sent to the United States to help train their newly raised armies in the British system of bayonet fighting. The British system of instruction, and the instructors themselves, were so well received by the Americans that when they were sent to France many of the American divisions took their AGS instructors with them. The following year a second group of instructors was sent to the United States, headed by Captain Harry Daniels VC MC, whose spirit and attitude towards the work ensured that this visit was equally successful.[4]

Issued with Army Orders dated 1st December, 1916.

47 / 618

BAYONET TRAINING.

1916.

Issued by the General Staff.

1916.

LONDON:
PUBLISHED BY HIS MAJESTY'S STATIONERY OFFICE,

To be purchased through any Bookseller or directly from
H.M. STATIONERY OFFICE at the following addresses:
IMPERIAL HOUSE, KINGSWAY. LONDON, W.C., and 28, ABINGDON STREET. LONDON, S.W.;
37, PETER STREET, MANCHESTER; 1. ST. ANDREW'S CRESCENT, CARDIFF;
23, FORTH STREET, EDINBURGH;
or from E. PONSONBY, LTD., 116, GRAFTON STREET, DUBLIN;
or from the Agencies in the British Colonies and Dependencies,
the United States of America and other Foreign Countries of
T. FISHER UNWIN, LTD., LONDON, W.C.

Price Twopence Net.

This Manual is issued by command of the Army Council for the guidance of all concerned.

R. H. Brade

WAR OFFICE,
   21*st November*, 1916.

(B 12502) Wt. 41489—367 280M 12/16 H & S P. 16/868 (*S*)

TABLE OF CONTENTS.

(B 12502)   A 2

BAYONET TRAINING, 1916.

(PROVISIONAL.)

SECTION 1.

SPECIAL FEATURES OF THE BAYONET.

1. To attack with the bayonet effectively requires **Good Direction, Strength and Quickness,** during a state of wild excitement and probably physical exhaustion. The limit of the range of a bayonet is about 5 feet (measured from the opponent's eyes), but more often the killing is at close quarters, at a range of 2 feet or less, when troops are struggling *corps à corps* in trenches or darkness.

The bayonet is essentially an offensive weapon—go straight at an opponent with the point threatening his throat and deliver the point wherever an opening presents itself. If no opening is obvious, one must be created by beating off the opponent's weapon or making a "feint point" in order to make him uncover himself.

2. Hand-to-hand fighting with the bayonet is individual, which means that a man must think and act for himself and rely on his own resource and skill; but, as in games, he must play for his side and not only for himself. In a bayonet assault all ranks go forward to kill or be killed, and only those who have developed skill and strength by constant training will be able to kill.

3. The spirit of the bayonet must be inculcated into all

(B 12502)   B

ranks so that they go forward with that aggressive determination and confidence of superiority born of continual practice, without which a bayonet assault will not be effective.

4. The technical points of bayonet fighting are extremely few and simple The essence of bayonet training is continuity of practice.

SECTION 2.

METHOD OF CARRYING OUT BAYONET TRAINING AND HINTS TO INSTRUCTORS.

5. An important point to be kept in mind in bayonet training is the development of the individual by teaching him to think and act for himself. The simplest means of attaining this end is to make men use their brains and eyes to the fullest extent by carrying out the practices, so far as possible, without words of command, *i.e.*, to point at a shifting target as soon as it is stationary, to parry sticks, &c. The class should, whenever possible, work in pairs and act on the principle of "Master and Pupil." This procedure, in itself, develops individuality and confidence. Sharp jerky words of command, which tend to make men act mechanically, should be omitted. Rapidity of movement and alertness are taught by competition in fixing and unfixing the bayonet and by other such "quickening movements."

6. As the technique of bayonet fighting is so simple, long detail is quite unnecessary and makes the work monotonous. All instruction should be carried out on common sense lines. It should seldom be necessary to give the detail of a "point" or "parry" more than two or three times, after which the classes should acquire the correct positions by practice. For

this reason a lesson or daily practice should rarely last more than half-an-hour. Remember that nothing kills interest so easily as monotony.

7. The spirit of the bayonet is to be inculcated by describing the special features of bayonet and hand-to-hand fighting. The men must learn to practise bayonet fighting in the spirit and with the enthusiasm which animate them when training for their games, and to look upon their instructor as a trainer and helper.

8. Interest in the work is to be created by explaining the reasons for the various positions, the method of handling the rifle and bayonet, and the uses of the "points." Questions should be put to the men to find out whether they understand these reasons. When men realise the object of their work they naturally take a greater interest in it.

9. Progression in bayonet training is regulated by obtaining first correct positions and good direction, then quickness. Strength is the outcome of continual practice.

10. In order to encourage dash and gradually strengthen the leg muscles from the commencement of the training, classes should be frequently practised in charging short distances.

11. All company officers and N.C.Os. should be taught how to instruct in bayonet training in order that they may be able to teach their platoons and sections this very important part of a soldier's training, which must be regularly practised during the whole of his service at home, and during his periods of rest behind the firing line.

12. Sacks for dummies should be filled with vertical layers of straw and thin sods (grass or heather), leaves, shavings, &c., in such a way as to give the greatest resistance without injury to the bayonet. A realistic effect, necessitating a strong withdrawal as if gripped by a bone, is obtained by

(B 12502)   B 2

inserting a vertical layer of pieces of hard wood, $\frac{1}{4}$-inch thick, (old cheese cases, oak palings, &c.), between the stuffing and the sack on the side facing the attacker; only one layer of wood is to be used, and the grain must be vertical.

These sack dummies can be made to stand on end by fixing a wooden cross or star (two or three pieces of wood about 2 inches broad and $\frac{3}{4}$ inch thick nailed across one another) in the base of the sack before filling it. They can also be placed with good effect on rough tripods, or tied to improvised stools. Dummy sacks should be hung from gallows by a double suspension from the cross-bar to the top corners and weighted or tethered to the ground from the bottom corners.

13. The greatest care should be taken that the object representing the opponent and its support should be incapable of injuring the bayonet or butt. Only light sticks are to be used for parrying practice.

The chief causes of injury to the bayonet are insufficient instruction in the bayonet training lessons, failure to withdraw the bayonet clear of the dummy before advancing, and placing the dummies on hard unprepared ground.

14. The upkeep and proper filling of dummies, and the repair of assault practice courses, form part of the duties of Army Gymnastic Staff and Assistant Instructors.

15. For practising direction there must always be an aiming mark on the dummy. Cardboard discs for this purpose are supplied by the Stationery Office. By continually changing the position of the mark the " life " of the dummies is considerably prolonged. Should the supply of discs fail, they can be improvised out of cardboard or thick paper, or five or six numbers can be painted on the dummies as marks.

SECTION 3.

Preliminary Bayonet Lessons.

16. Open ranks for bayonet practice as follows :—"Rear Rank—About turn"; "Odd numbers of the front rank and even numbers of the rear rank—Six (or more) paces forward —March," "About turn"; "The whole, one pace right close—March." Or, "For Bayonet practice open—out."

Small classes should be opened out from single rank.

Classes should always work with bayonets fixed.

When teaching a new position, face the class to a flank and let them "rest." First show them the position, explaining essential points and giving the reasons for them. Then show the position a second time, making the class observe each movement, so that, from the very commencement of the bayonet training, a man is taught to use his eyes and brain. Face the ranks and order them to assume the position explained and shown. Pick out the man who shows the best position and let the class look at and copy him. Remember that his position may not be ideal, but it is more correct than those assumed by the remainder, who, being beginners, cannot distinguish the difference between a good position and an ideal one. Many instructors err by trying to get a class of beginners to idealise at once.

17. The Recruit's Course consists of five lessons and the Final Assault Practice. The hours in the syllabus for bayonet training are so divided as to give daily practice. The training should be carried out chiefly in a "free and easy" kit, but men should be accustomed to use their bayonets when wearing belt and pouches, and packs may be worn when an efficiency test is in progress. For the "pointing" and "parrying" practices a light stick, 5 feet to 5 feet 9 inches long and 1¾ inches to 3 inches in circumference, with thrusting ring and pad, must be provided for every two men.

18. Half-an-hour a day, on at least five days a week, should be devoted to the daily practice in bayonet fighting by trained soldiers. By this daily practice accuracy of direction, quickness, and strength are developed, and a soldier is accustomed to using the bayonet under conditions which approximate to actual fighting. This half-hour should be apportioned to (1) Pointing at the body; (2) Pointing at thrusting rings, &c., on light sticks at varying distances and directions; (3) Parrying light sticks; (4) Dummy work; and (5), when sufficiently proficient, the Final Assault Practice.

Lesson 1.

19. Point of the bayonet directed at the base of the opponent's throat, the rifle held easily and naturally with both hands, the barrel inclined slightly (about 30°) to the left, the right hand, over the navel, grasping the small of the butt, the left hand holding the rifle at the most convenient position in front of the backsight so that the left arm is only slightly bent, *i.e.*, the upper arm and fore-arm making an angle of about 150°. The legs well separated in a natural position, such as a man walking might adopt on meeting with resistance, *i.e.*, left knee slightly bent, right foot flat on the ground with toe inclined to the right front.

The position should not be constrained in any way but be one of aggression, alertness, and readiness to go forward for immediate attack (*vide* Plate I).

The "On guard" position will also be taught with the right foot in front.

Common Faults.

(1) Leaning body back.
(2) Left arm too much bent.
(3) Right hand held too low and too far back.
(4) Rifle grasped too rigidly, restraining all freedom of movement.

Assume a position of " rest " in the easiest way without moving the feet.

The hands holding the rifle as when on guard ; the left wrist level with, and directly in front of, the left shoulder ; right hand level with and to the right of the buckle of the waist-belt.

When jumping ditches, surmounting obstacles, &c., the position of the rifle should be approximately maintained with the left hand alone, leaving the right hand free.

20. Grasping the rifle firmly, vigorously deliver the point from the " on guard " position to the full extent of the left arm, butt running alongside and kept close to the right forearm. Body inclined forward ; left knee well bent ; right leg braced, and weight of the body pressed well forward with the fore part of the right foot, heel raised.

The chief power in a " point " is derived from the right arm with the weight of the body behind it, the left arm being used more to direct the point of the bayonet. The eyes must be fixed on the object at which the point is directed. In making " points " other than straight to the front, the left foot should move laterally in the same direction as that in which the " point " is made.

During the later stages of this lesson the men should be practised in stepping forward with the rear foot when delivering the " point."

Common Faults.

(1) Rifle drawn back before delivering the " point."
(2) Butt of the rifle held as high as or against the right shoulder.
(3) The eyes not directed on the object.
(4) Left knee not sufficiently bent.
(5) Body not thrust sufficiently forward.

Remarks.

The " long point " is made against an opponent at a range of about four to five feet from the attacker's eye.

21. To withdraw the bayonet after a " long point " has been delivered, draw the rifle straight back until the right hand is well behind the hip, and immediately resume the " on guard " position. If the leverage or proximity to the object transfixed renders it necessary, the left hand must first be slipped up close to the piling-swivel, and, when a pupil reaches the stage of delivering a " point " while advancing on a dummy, he will adopt this method.

After every " point," a rapid " withdrawal," essential to quick work with the bayonet, should be practised before returning to the " on guard " position.

Progression.

22. Men should always be made to point at a target, e.g., at a named part of the body of the opposite man : " At the right eye" (long pause to commence with), "point" (a pause), " withdraw." Oblique " points " should be practised by pointing at the men to the right and left fronts.

As progress is made, the pause between the " point" and the " withdrawal " should be shortened until the men reach a stage when they " withdraw " and come " on guard " directly after making a " point," judging their own time. They should be taught to point at two or more parts of the body, *e.g.*, " First at the nose, then at the right thigh— point."

To practise action against a retreating foe, turn the inside ranks about and let them " rest." Show the position of the kidneys (small of the back, either side of the spine), and make the outside ranks point at those of the inside ranks, and *vice versâ*.

23. If possible, the point of the bayonet should be directed against an opponent's throat, especially in *corps á corps* fighting, as the point will enter easily and make a fatal wound on penetrating a few inches and, being near the eyes, makes an opponent " funk." Other vulnerable and usually exposed parts are the face, chest, lower abdomen and thighs, and the region of the kidneys when the back is turned. Four to six inches' penetration is sufficient to incapacitate and allow for a quick withdrawal, whereas if a bayonet is driven home too far it is often impossible to withdraw it. In such cases a round should be fired to break up the obstruction.

24. The class, working in pairs, with the Instructor supervising, should be practised in pointing in various directions, *e.g.*, (1) at the opposite man's hand, which he places in various positions on and off his body ; (2) at thrusting rings, &c., tied on the ends of sticks.

This practice should be done without word of command, so that the eye and brain may be trained.

25. The men will be taught to transfix a disc or number painted on a dummy, first at a distance of about five feet from the dummy (*i.e.*, the extreme range of the bayonet), and then after advancing three or more paces. The advance

(B 12502)   C .

must be made in a practical and natural way, and should be practised with either foot to the front when the "point" is delivered.

The rifle must never be drawn back when making a "long point" in a forward movement. The impetus of the body and the forward stretching of the arms supply sufficient force.

The bayonet must be withdrawn immediately after the "point" has been delivered, and a forward threatening attitude be assumed to the side of or beyond the dummy.

Unless the rifle is firmly gripped it is liable to injure the hand.

To guard against accidents the men must be at least five feet apart when the practice is carried out collectively.

The principles of this practice will be observed when pointing at dummies in trenches, standing upright on the ground, or suspended on gallows. They should be applied at first slowly and deliberately, for **no attempt must be made to carry out the Final Assault Practice before the men have been carefully instructed in, and have thoroughly mastered, the preliminary lessons.**

Lesson 2.

The Right and Left Parry.

26. From the position of "On guard," vigorously straighten the left arm without bending the wrist or twisting the rifle in the hand, and force the rifle forward far enough to the right (left) to fend off the adversary's weapon.

The eyes must be kept on the weapon which is being parried.

Common Faults.

(1) Wide sweeping parry with no forward movement in it.

(2) Eyes taken off the weapon to be parried.

Men should be taught to regard the parry as part of an offensive movement, namely, of the "point" which would immediately follow it in actual combat. For this reason, as soon as the movements of the parries have been learnt they should always be accompanied with a slight forward movement of the body.

Parries will be practised with the right as well as with the left foot forward, preparatory to the practice of parrying when advancing.

27. Men when learning the parries should be made to observe the movements of the rifle carefully, and should not be kept longer at this practice than is necessary for them to understand what is required, that is vigorous, yet controlled, action.

The class works in pairs with scabbards on bayonets, one man pointing with the stick and the other parrying; the "on-guard" position is resumed after each parry. At first this practice must be slow and deliberate, without being allowed to become mechanical, and will be progressively increased in rapidity and vigour.

Later a "point" at that part of the body indicated by the opposite man's hand should immediately follow the parry; and, finally, sticks long enough to represent the opponent's weapon in the "on-guard" position should be attached to the dummies and parried before delivering the "point."

The men must also be taught to parry points made at them :—(1) by an "enemy" in a trench when they are them-

(B 12502)   c 2

selves on the parapet ; (2) by an "enemy" on the parapet when they are in the trench, and ; (3) when both are fighting on the same level at close quarters in a deep trench.

Lesson 3.

The Short Point.

28. Shift the left hand quickly towards the muzzle and draw the rifle back to the full extent of the right arm, the butt either upwards or downwards according as a low or a high point is to be made ; then deliver the "point" vigorously to the full extent of the left arm.

N.B.—The "short point" is used at a range of about three feet, and in close fighting it is the natural "point" to make when the bayonet has just been withdrawn after a "long point." If a strong "withdrawal" is necessary the right hand should be slipped above the backsight after the "short point" has been made.

29. The principles of the three practices of Lesson 1 should be observed so far as they apply. By placing two discs on a dummy the "short point" should be taught in conjunction with the "long point," the first disc being transfixed with the latter, the second with the former point. On delivery of the "long point" if the left foot is forward, the "short point" would take place with the right foot forward, and *vice versâ*.

Parries will be practised from the position of the "short point."

Lesson 4.

Jab or Upward Point.

30. From the position of the "short point" shift the right hand up the rifle and grasp it above the backsight, at the same time bringing the rifle to an almost vertical position close to the body, and, from this position, bend the knees and jab the point of the bayonet upwards into the throat or under the chin of the opponent.

Common Faults.

(1) Rifle drawn backward and not held upright enough.

(2) Rifle grasped too low with the right hand.

From the "jab" position men will be practised in fending off an attack made on any part of them by an opponent.

When making a "jab" from the "on guard" position, the right, being the thrusting hand, will be brought up first.

The jab can be employed successfully in close-quarter fighting in narrow trenches and when "embraced" by an opponent.

Lesson 5.

Methods of Injuring an Opponent.

31. It should be impressed upon the class that, although a man's "point" has missed or has been parried, or his bayonet has been broken, he can, as "attacker," still maintain his advantage by injuring his opponent in one of the ways described in paras. 32–35.

32. Butt Stroke I.—Swing the butt up at the opponent's fork, ribs, forearm, &c., using a half arm blow and advancing the rear foot.

Butt Stroke II.—If the opponent jumps back so that the first butt stroke misses, the rifle will come into horizontal position over the left shoulder, butt leading ; the attacker will then step in with the rear foot and dash the butt into his opponent's face.

Butt Stroke III.—If the opponent retires still further out of distance, the attacker again closes up and slashes his bayonet down on his opponent's head or neck.

Butt Stroke IV.—If the point is beaten or brought down, the butt can be used effectively by crashing it down on the opponent's head with an over-arm blow, advancing the rear foot. When the opponent is out of distance, Butt Stroke III can again be used.

In individual fighting the butt can also be used horizontally against the opponent's ribs, forearm, &c. This method is impossible in trench fighting or in an attack, owing to the horizontal sweep of the bayonet to the attacker's left.

It should be clearly understood that the butt must not be employed when it is possible to use the point of the bayonet effectively.

33. Butt Stroke I is essentially a half-arm blow from the shoulder, keeping the elbow rigid, and it can, therefore, be successfully employed only when the right hand is grasping the rifle at the small of the butt.

34. Butt strokes can only be used in certain circumstances and positions, but if men acquire absolute control of their weapons under these conditions they will be able to adapt themselves to all other phases of in-fighting. For instance, when a man is gripped by an opponent so that neither the point nor the butt can be used, the knee brought up against the fork or the heel stamped on the instep may momentarily disable him and make him release his hold.

35. When wrestling, the opponent can be tripped by forcing his weight on to one leg and kicking that leg away from under him, or any other wrestler's trip, *e.g.*, "back-heel," may be used.

N.B.—The above methods will only temporarily disable an enemy, who must be killed with the bayonet.

36. When the classes have been shown the methods of using the butt and the knee they should be practised on the padded stick, *e.g.*, fix several discs on a dummy and make a point at one, use the knee on another fixed low down, jab a third, and so on.

Light dummies should be used for practice with the butt, in order to avoid damage to it.

SECTION 4.

TACTICAL APPLICATION OF THE BAYONET.

37. A bayonet assault should preferably be made under cover of fire, surprise, or darkness. In these circumstances the prospect of success is greatest, for a bayonet is useless at any range except hand-to-hand.

38. At night all these forms of cover can be utilised. On the other hand, confusion is inherent in fighting by night ; consequently, the execution of a successful night attack with the bayonet requires considerable and lengthy training. Units should be frequently practised in night work with the bayonet.

39. The bayonet is essentially a weapon of offence which must be used with skill and vigour ; otherwise it has but little effect. To await passively an opportunity of using the bayonet entails defeat, since an approaching enemy will merely stand out of bayonet range and shoot down the defenders.

40. In an assault the enemy should be killed with the bayonet. Firing should be avoided, for in the mix-up a bullet, after passing through an opponent's body, may kill a friend who happens to be in the line of fire.

Final Assault Practice.

41. This practice is only to be carried out after the men have been thoroughly trained in all the preliminary lessons, and have acquired complete control of their weapons, otherwise injury to rifles and bayonets will result from improper application of the methods laid down in the foregoing instruction.

The Final Assault Practice must approximate as nearly as possible to the conditions of actual fighting.

Nervous tension due to the anticipation of an attack, reacting on the body, as well as the advance across the open and the final dash at the enemy, combine to tire an assaulting party. It is only by their physical fitness and superior skill in the use of the bayonet that they can overcome a comparatively fresh foe.

Therefore quick aim and good direction of the bayonet, when moving rapidly or even when surmounting obstacles, accurate delivery of a point of sufficient strength and vigour to penetrate clothing and equipment, clean withdrawal of the bayonet—which requires no small effort, especially should it be fixed by a bone—are of the greatest importance, and need the same careful attention and constant practice as are devoted to obtaining efficiency with the rifle.

In the Final Assault Practice the charge brings the men to the first trench in a comparatively exhausted condition, and the accuracy of the aim is tested by the disc, which can only be "carried" by a true and vigorous thrust and a clean withdrawal.

For this practice the men should be made to begin the assault from a trench six or seven feet deep, as well as from the open, and they should not cheer until close up to the "enemy."

42. A reproduction of a labyrinth of trenches, with dummies in the "dug-outs" and shelters between the trenches, forms an excellent Final Assault Practice Course. Assaults should be made from all four sides in order to give variety. The edges of the trenches should be protected by spars or baulks anchored back ; otherwise constant use will soon wear them out. Cinders scattered over the course prevent the men from slipping. If gallows cannot be erected, sack dummies should be placed on tripods or on end, as well as lying in trenches or on the parapets, with soft earth free from stones under them.

Commanding Officers will be responsible for the construction of the Final Assault Practice Courses, and will decide on the number, length, and nature of the trenches in accordance with the ground available. Officers in charge of Physical and Bayonet Training, or where there are no such officers Army Gymnastic Staff and Assistant Instructors, will be responsible to Commanding Officers for the upkeep of the courses.

43. Extremely interesting and practical schemes in trench warfare can be arranged by combining the Final Assault Practice with other branches of training, *e.g.*, bombing, laying sandbags, entrenching.

44. Competitions can be arranged by allotting or deducting marks for (1) number of discs transfixed and carried on a bayonet, (2) time taken from giving the signal to charge until the last man of the team passes the finishing post, and (3) style.

Competitions should never be carried out until the men have completed their lessons in bayonet training and thoroughly mastered the handling of the bayonet in the Final Assault Practice.

SECTION 5.

TACTICAL PRINCIPLES TO BE OBSERVED DURING BAYONET TRAINING.

METHOD OF CARRYING RIFLE WITH BAYONET FIXED.

45. *Quick Short Advance* (in the open).

The rifle will be held at the "High Port."

This position is suitable for close formation, minimises risk of accidents when surmounting obstacles, and can be maintained with the left hand alone, allowing free use of the right when necessary.

46. *Long Advance* (close formation).

The rifle will be slung over the left shoulder, sling to the front and perpendicular to the ground.

This is a safe method of carrying the rifle and allowing the free use of both hands.

47. *Long Advance* (open order).

The rifle will be carried at "the trail."

THE ASSAULT.

48. The importance of discipline and organised control throughout the conduct of a bayonet assault cannot be over emphasised. It must be remembered that in this, as in all other military operations, success can only be achieved through the closest co-operation of all concerned ; and that, while individual initiative is not to be discouraged, it must be strictly subordinated to the intention of the leader of the assaulting party.

Men should be shown by demonstration that it is in their

own interests to pay attention to this point, and that the failure of an enterprise can usually be traced to the lack of this close co-operation.

49. During training the following general principles will be observed :—

i. All members of the attacking party must leave the trench or rise from cover simultaneously.

In addition to the advantages of surprise needless casualties are thereby avoided.

ii. The first stage, especially of a long advance, will be slow and steady—not faster than the pace of the slowest man.

Such an advance has a decided moral effect on the enemy, makes certain of the maximum shock at the moment of impact, and at the same time allows the attacking force to reach its objective without undue exhaustion. On the other hand, if the assault is allowed to develop without control and in a haphazard fashion, the moral effect of a steady resistless wall of men is lost, and the defenders may be given time to dispose of their opponents in detail.

50. The actual charge will not be made over a greater distance than twenty paces. Within the last ten yards and before closing with the enemy the rifle will be brought to the threatening, yet defensive, "on guard." Line will as far as possible be maintained until actual contact with the enemy is gained.

51. As soon as the position has been taken, and prior to any attack on a further position or any other operation whatsoever, the infantry must be reformed as explained in Infantry Training, Section **124**, 4, ammunition being redistributed and every precaution being taken against a counter-attack. In trench warfare indiscriminate pursuit with the bayonet must never be allowed unless orders to that effect have been given by the leader of the assaulting party. The attacking troops are not so fresh as the enemy, and experience has shown that unorganised pursuit lends itself to ambush and casualties from machine gun fire. In most cases the work of immediate pursuit is better done by the supporting artillery—the infantry assisting by rapid fire on the retreating enemy.

Assault Practice.

52. A useful form of Final Assault Practice which can be adapted to a variety of "special ideas" is described in paras. 53–55.

The following materials are assumed :—

A. Communicating trenches leading to a fire trench with an open space in front.

B. An occupied enemy trench.

C. Gallows with dummies, representing the enemy,

      (i) retiring from " B," or

     (ii) coming up in support of " B," or

    (iii) making a counter-attack on the captured trench " B."

53. (i) The attacking party makes a controlled assault on " A," which is cleared of the enemy.

(ii) It is then reformed and an assault is launched on " B," after taking which

(iii) " C " is regarded in one or other of the above ways, and action taken accordingly.

54. Throughout the training men must be constantly practised in :—

i. The recognised method of carrying the rifle with bayonet fixed.

ii. Rapid advance out of deep trenches.

iii. Control and maintenance of line and opening of fire during an advance.

iv. Using the bayonet with effect in the cramped space of communicating and fire trenches.

v. Reforming and opening of fire after the assault.

vi. Acting as leaders of attacking party.

55. Instructors should endeavour by every means in their power to arouse the interest and imagination of their men during the assault practice. The "special idea" to be adopted should invariably be explained beforehand.

Each dummy must be regarded as an actual armed opponent, and each line of dummies as an enemy line attacking, defending or retiring, and be disposed of accordingly.

Any tendency towards carelessness and slackness must be instantly checked, and it should be impressed on all ranks that a practice assault which is not carried out with the necessary quickness, vigour and determination is worse than useless.

Lack of imagination, which allows men and their leaders to violate the most elementary principles of tactics in practice assaults against dummies, can only lead to disaster in a real assault against the enemy.

SECTION 6.

GENERAL INSTRUCTIONS FOR BAYONET TRAINING PRACTICE.

(*a*) "On guard," "withdraw," all points and parries, and the "jab," will be taught first with the left, then with the right foot forward.

(*b*) The "starting position" for a "short point" is shown

in Plate IV. All "short points" will be practised from this position, which must be marked, except after a "point" into a dummy, by a momentary pause so as to break men of the habit of drawing back the rifle from "on guard" before making a "point."

(c) From the outset squads will be frequently practised in charging for short distances in the open —as a strengthening exercise for the legs and a quickening exercise.

(d) A target to point at will always be named when working by word of command ; it will be indicated by the position of the hand when working in class ; and it will be clearly marked on all dummies.

(e) When working in ranks the distance apart must be sufficient to avoid all danger of accident when the "points" are being made. When "points" have been made advancing, the ranks will change position by coming to the "high port," doubling past each other right shoulder to right shoulder, and turning about. When working against dummies, men will always continue the movement past the dummy, which they will leave on their right.

(f) The "withdrawal," once taught, will be made after each "point." After a "point," advancing rear foot or on the advance, the hand will always be moved up the rifle, but in the 1st and 2nd practices, since the arm and body are already stretched to their full extent, and the left hand cannot move further forward, the hand will be shifted after the "withdrawal" from the "long point."

(g) All sticks must be padded at one end.

(h) In the third practices the "points" will also be practised deliberately and progressively on dummies placed, as a preparation for the Final Assault Course, in positions of increasing difficulty, e.g., on parapets and steps of shallow trenches, and in fire and communicating trenches.

(*i*) Scabbards will not be removed from the bayonet except for pointing at dummies.

SECTION 7.

(1) Class arrangements.
(2) Explain hand-to-hand fighting and inculcate the spirit of the bayonet.

LESSON 1.

(3) On guard.   (Plate I.)
(4) Rest.
(5) High port.

1st Practice.   (In class, by word of command.)

   (6) " Long point."
   (7) " Withdrawal "; (*a*) after stationary "point"; (*b*) after " point " advancing rear foot (Plate III).   (First demonstrated by Instructor on a dummy.)
   (8) Oblique " long point."
   (9) " Long point," followed by " long point " advancing rear foot.
  (10) Vulnerable spots explained ; region of the kidneys shown ; class practised in making " points " at these.

2nd Practice.   (Class working by eye.)

  (11) " Long point."
  (12) " Long point," followed by " long point " advancing rear foot.

(13) Varied direct and oblique "long points" at thrusting ring.

3rd Practice. (Pointing at dummy.)

(14) "Long point" (Plate II).
(15) "Long point" advancing rear foot.
(16) Advance, "long point."
(17) Advance, "long points" (at two or more dummies).

LESSON 2.

(18) Explain value of parries : how, in charging, the parry must be strong enough to beat aside opponent's weapon.

1st Practice. (In class, by word of command.)

(19) Explain, and make the class perform, the movements required for the various parries.

2nd Practice. (Class working by eye.)

(20) Parry stick pointed at the breast.
(21) Parry stick pointed at the breast and point.
(22) Parry stick pointed at head, body or legs.
(23) Parry stick pointed in varying order at head, body or legs, and point.
(24) When standing in a trench, parry "point" made with stick from above.
(25) When standing on a parapet, parry "point" made with stick by man in trench.
(26) With stick parry "point" made with stick by advancing opponent.
(27) With stick parry "point" made with stick by advancing opponent, and point.

(28) With stick, parry "point" made with stick lightly held in one hand by charging opponent. (By holding his stick in right or left hand the attacker will clearly show on which side he is pointing, and he will pass on that flank.)

3rd Practice. (Pointing at dummy with stick representing opponent's weapon.)

(29) Advance, parry stick and point.

Lesson 3.

(30) Demonstrate "short point," and explain when it is used (Plate IV).

1st Practice. (In class, by word of command.)

(31) "Short point."
(32) "Withdrawal"; (*a*) stationary; (*b*) advancing rear foot. (Demonstrated by Instructor on dummy.)
(33) Oblique "short point."
(34) "Short point" advancing rear foot.
(35) "Long point" advancing rear foot, followed by "short point" advancing rear foot.

2nd Practice. (Class working by eye.)

(36) "Short point."
(37) "Short point" advancing rear foot.
(38) "Long point" advancing rear foot, followed by "short point" advancing rear foot.
(39) Varied direct and oblique "long and short points" at thrusting ring.
(40) Practise various parries, parries and "points," from "short point" position.

3rd Practice. (Pointing at dummy.)

(41) "Short point."

(42) "Short point" advancing rear foot.

(43) "Long point" advancing rear foot ; "short point" advancing rear foot.

(44) Advance, "long point," "short point" (at two dummies in suitable positions).

LESSON 4.

(45) Demonstrate "jab" at dummy : then, by placing men of the squad in suitable positions, explain when and how it is used in conjunction with "points" (Plate V).

1st Practice. (In class, by word of command.)

(46) "Jab," from "jab" position.

(47) "Short point" advancing rear foot, "jab" advancing rear foot.

(48) "Long point" advancing rear foot, "jab" advancing rear foot.

(49) "Long point" advancing rear foot, "short point" advancing rear foot, "jab" advancing rear foot.

(50) "Short point" advancing rear foot, "jab" advancing rear foot, "long point" advancing rear foot.

2nd Practice. (Class working by eye.)

(51) "Jab" at thrusting ring (Plate VI).

(52) Direct and oblique "long and short points," and "jabs," in varying order, at thrusting ring.

(53) When in "jab" position, fend off high and low "points" made with stick.

3rd Practice. (Pointing at dummy.)

(54) "Jab" from "jab" position.

(55) "Short point" advancing rear foot, and "jab" advancing rear foot.

(56) "Long point" advancing rear foot, "short point" advancing rear foot, and "jab" advancing rear foot (at dummies).

(57) Advance, "long point" and "jab."

(58) Advance, "long point, "short point," and two or more "jabs" (at dummies).

Lesson 5.

1st Practice. (Word of command.)

(59) Class to practise butt stroke I.

(60) „   ,   „   II.

(61) „   „   „   III.

(62) „   „   „   IV.

2nd Practice. (Working by eye.)

(63) Butt stroke I at padded stick (Plate VII).

(64)   „   II   „   „

(65)   „   III   „   „

(66)   „   IV   „   „   (Plate VIII).

(67) Repeat in varying order.

(68) "Long points," "short points," and "jabs," at thrusting ring, with butt strokes at padded stick, varied.

(69) Trips practised by men working in pairs.

3rd Practice. (On dummy.)

(70) "Point," "jab," &c., at dummies, followed by butt strokes I to IV at light dummies, and introducing kicks and any other form of in-fighting.

SECTION 8.

A GUIDE FOR THE TRAINED SOLDIER'S DAILY PRACTICE.
(Half-Hour.)

(1) (5 minutes).

      (*a*) "Long points" at hand ; Summary (11), (12).
         (Not more than 8 " points " each man.)

      (*b*) "Short points" at hand ; Summary (36), (37),
         (38). (Not more than 10 " points " each man.)

(2) (5 minutes.) Steady advance over obstacles and charge 20 yards—about 100 yards in all.

(3) (4 minutes.) Parrying stick and pointing ; Summary (23).

(4) (4 minutes.) Butt strokes, each stroke twice ; Summary (59), (60), (61), (62) ; or practise trips, &c. ; Summary (69).

(5) (6 minutes.) "Long points," "short points," and "jabs," at thrusting ring, with butt strokes at pad, varied ; Summary (68).

(6) (6 minutes.) Final Assault Practice.

PLATE I. "ON GUARD." LESSON 1 ; SUMMARY (3).

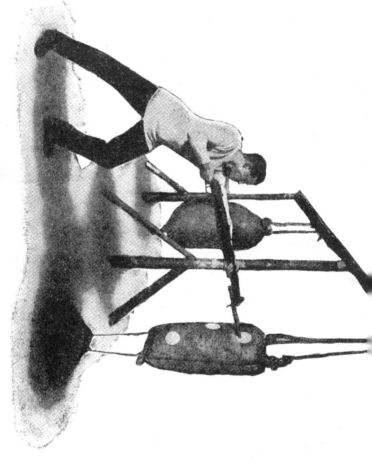

PLATE II. "LONG POINT." LESSON I ; SUMMARY (14).

PLATE III. "WITHDRAWAL." LESSON 1; SUMMARY (7), (b).

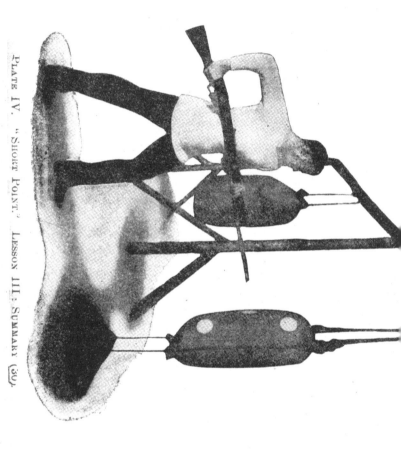

PLATE IV. "SHORT POINT." LESSON III. SUMMARY (30).

PLATE V. "JAB." LESSON IV ; SUMMARY (45) & (56).

PLATE VI. "JAB" AT THRUSTING RING. LESSON IV; SUMMARY (51).

122

PLATE VII. BUTT STROKE 1. LESSON V; SUMMARY (63).

PLATE VIII. BUTT STROKE IV. LESSON V ; SUMMARY (66).

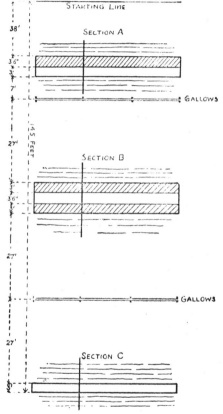

Diagram 1.—Type of Simple "Final Assault Practice"
It is attacked both ways, and the positions

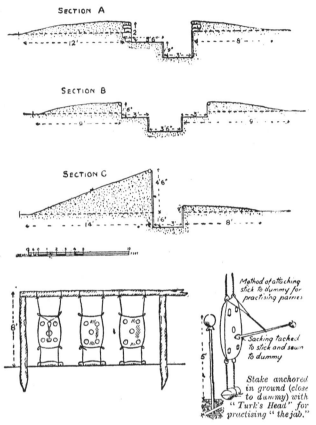

SECTION A

SECTION B

SECTION C

Method of attaching stick to dummy for practising parries

Sacking tacked to stick and sewn to dummy

Stake anchored in ground (close to dummy) with "Turk's Head" for practising "the jab."

Course used at the Hd.-Qrs. Gymnasium, Aldershot.

of the trench sack dummies are varied.

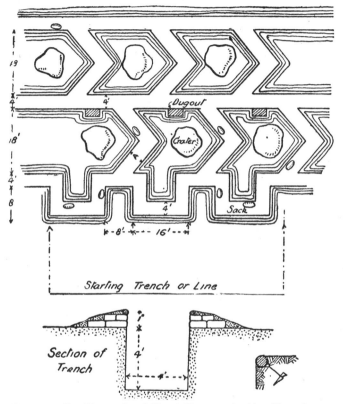

Diagram 2.—Example of Short Communication Trenches.

Which should form part of the usual Final Assault Practice course, where, owing to lack of ground, a "labyrinth" for daily practice with the bayonet in the confined space of a trench cannot be constructed within a convenient distance. On arrival in France drafts are tested in trench bayonet work.

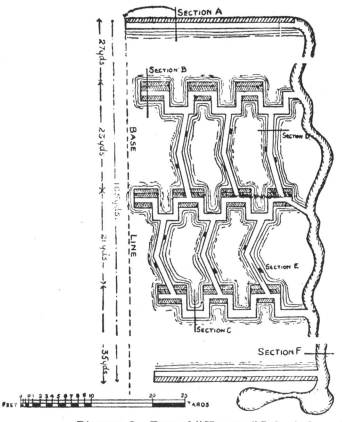

Diagram 3.—Type of "Nursery" Labyrinth used

The positions of the sack dummies are frequently changed.   The ground
the men practised in clearing such "cramped"

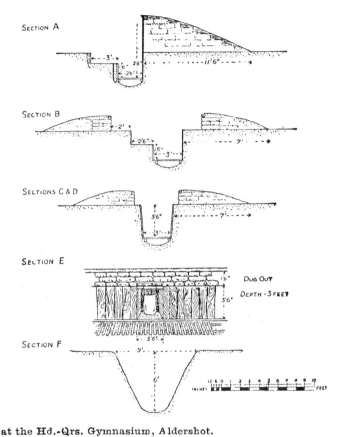

SECTION A

SECTION B

SECTIONS C & D

SECTION E

DUG OUT

DEPTH · 3 FEET

SECTION F

at the Hd.-Qrs. Gymnasium, Aldershot.

between the trenches is pitted with "craters" containing dummies, and
ground as well as in clearing the trenches.

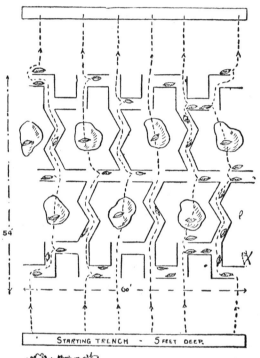

STARTING TRENCH - 5 FEET DEEP.

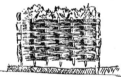

Diagram 4. — "Overground Labyrinth" for Practice in Wet Weather.

It can be constructed with six-foot hurdles, or canvas screens, or any materials which will give the approximate shape and the narrow limits of trenches. The example above requires 102 six-foot hurdles, which may be set up on fresh ground, and also made to represent various schemes of trenches. The sack dummies should be placed in such a position that the attacker does not see them until he is upon them. Six extra communicating trenches may take the place of craters.

Fig. 5.—Parrying-stick with "Thrusting Ring" and "Pad."

For use :—

(a) On the "master and pupil" principle, for practising in two ranks the "Long Point," "Short Point," and "Jab," according to the position of the ring, alternating with butt strokes and kicks at the pad, according to its position.

(b) In charging practice, when both ranks, extended to 3 yards' interval and 20 yards' distance, use the padded ends. Men of one rank charge at a steady double and "point" at opposite men, who "parry." Charging rank halts 20 yards beyond, turns about and charges again, the other rank facing about to meet it. The slight lateral movement required to "parry" is clearly demonstrated in this practice.

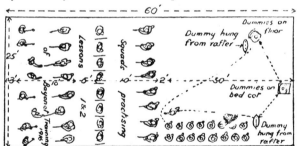

Diagram 6.—Plan of Distribution of Bayonet Training
Squads in a Barrack-room in Wet Weather.

Sack dummies can be hung from rafters or frames constructed for the purpose, or be laid *two deep* on bed cots or upon the floor

Printed under the authority of His Majesty's Stationery Office
By HARRISON AND SONS,
PRINTERS IN ORDINARY TO HIS MAJESTY,
ST. MARTIN'S LANE, LONDON, W.C.

5

The 'Spirit of the Bayonet'

Major R. B. Campbell was a superb lecturer, charismatic and possessing a strong physical presence, with broken nose and battered ears. His lectures would resemble a practical demonstration. By pulling no punches, with his enthusiasm he could whip the troops into a 'frenzied hate against the enemy'.[1] He would address troops, sometimes a brigade strong, in the open air in an attempt to stimulate their fighting spirit.

The following excerpt from Siegfried Sassoon's *Memoirs of an Infantry Officer* provides a classic example of how Campbell tone would captivate his audience:

> The bullet and the bayonet are brother and sister – if you do not kill him he will kill you. Stick him between the eyes, in the throat, in the chest – do not waste good steel – six inches are enough. What is the good of a foot of steel sticking out of a man's neck. Three inches will do for him – when he coughs, go look for another – kill them! Kill them! There is only one good Bosche and that is a dead one.[2]

Although Campbell was a great advocate for using the bayonet, he only regarded it as a practical weapon in part, and later confided that it was a means of boosting the morale of war-weary troops:

> To be truthful, it was all a bit of ballyhoo. Even by 1914 the bayonet was obsolete. The number of men killed by the bayonet on the Western Front was very small, but it was superb as a morale booster. Get the bayonet in the hands of despondent troops and you can make tigers within hours. I found nothing better to introduce recruits to the terrible conditions which awaited the devils up the line.[3]

*

SPIRIT OF THE BAYONET

By

Lt Col R. B. Campbell
(*Circa* 1914–18)

Decisive Victory.
Decisive victory – the complete defeat of the enemy – can be
gained only by the personal contact of opposing forces, by hand-
to-hand fighting. If an army is broken by long-range fighting, it
will retire, consolidate its scattered forces and fight again: but,
if it is defeated in *'hand-to-hand combat'*, it will have had all
the fight knocked out of it and will become demoralized. Hand-
to-hand fighters are essential to the success of an army. If the
'Bosche' had had our cavalry at Mons, we should have been
wiped out. If he had had our infantry, with all its dash and
devil, at the first and second battles of Ypres, he would have
taken Calais. Fortunately, the *'Bosche'* is not a natural hand-to-
hand fighter. He dislikes the personal contact. He resembles the
boxer who has no *'knock-out'* punch. He has had us *'groggy'* on
several occasions, but he has always lacked the finishing touch.
He has no fondness for *'mixing'*. He is good at out-fighting, but
he is a bad in-fighter. If you match two men, equally skilful at
out-fighting, to fight to finish, which will win? Why the better
in-fighter of course.

Natural Fighting.
Who are the in-fighters of an army? The Infantry. To use another
simile, the Infantry are the forwards of the football team, who
dash in and score, and so complete the good work of the half-
backs and backs – the artillery and machine gunners. For this
reason the army which possesses the best natural fighters holds
an overwhelming advantage. What is the natural fighter? *What
is natural fighting?* It is the most primitive mode of fighting, the
fashion in which animals fight, the fighting of children whom
passion has deprived of reason; it is biting, fighting '*tooth to
tooth*'. All fighting is based upon '*tooth to tooth*' – contact –
fighting. As fighting departs from the natural, becomes artificial,
so the fighters get farther and farther apart.

What is the next stage from '*tooth to tooth*' fighting? Fighting with hands, fists and feet. Then weapons are introduced; first, the club, sword and spear; then the stone, thrown by hand or from a sling. From the sling to the bow and arrow is only one step, from bow and arrow to rifle. With each stage of evolution opponents are separated by greater and greater distances, until to-day, with long range artillery, they can no longer see each other.

Hand-to-hand Fighting.
A battle may begin out of sight, but how does it finish? By hand-to-hand fighting. One does not need to watch a modern battle to verify the truth of this. Have you ever seen two women fight? They may start fighting with their fists at arm's length range. But, which wins? The best biter, the best scratcher, the woman who wants to get to closer quarters, who wants to '*get there*'. It is the same with boys, fighting in parties, with stones. Which side wins? Not the boys who throw the farther, but the boys who are better with their fists, who are keen to get into it, to '*get-there*', the boys with the natural fighting spirit, the possession of which – the moral effect of which – means victory. Remember, the country which lengthens its weapons shortens its boundaries. What applies to woman and boys applies to armies in the field. Other things being equal, the army with the best natural fighters must win. The army which, while introducing long-range weapons, preserves the '*spirit of the bayonet*', is eager to use the bayonet, must win. Who tells us so? The '*Bosche*' himself. Here is an extract from the report of an examination of German Prisoners captured by the Fifth Army:

Admissions.

Bosche
The Report says:- 'The coolness and self-reliance of our men are much admired. (We must thank our games training for those qualities.) One German said that whatever else might be the relative merits of the two sides, *the English are much superior in bayonet fighting.* He commented sarcastically on the German eagerness to surrender as soon as their supply of hand grenades was exhausted and bayonet fighting resulted.' What does he say? He admits that we are the better contact fighter, the better natural fighters, in other words, that we must win. I do not mean to

imply that the *'Bosche'* is not a good fighter. On the contrary, he is. He is up to every trick of the trade, a trade of which he was accounted the leading exponent. He is a brave man too. But he is not an individual fighter. He relies upon his officers, his NCOs and his experts. He has drawn experts from every branch of science to assist him in the art of war. He relies so much upon science that he has lost sight of the fact that war is based upon, conditioned by, and limited by the human factor. The German soldier will fight like the Devil so long as he is under the control of his officers and experts, but, once their control is removed, he stops and becomes a *'hands-upper'*. The *'Bosche'* war-machine lacks the motor – the fighting spirit, which should keep it running when all its controllers are gone.

British Advantage.

To my mind, no army ever entered the field with such an advantage as ours. And that advantage is the British birth-right, the fighting spirit. It is in every *'Britisher'*. That fighting spirit, dormant sometimes, has been kept alive by our games, and to-day it is still the strongest passion of a *'Britisher'*. It is in every man. Watch the *'Britisher'* play football. If the other side scores, does he slacken? No, he fights on. If at half-time the other side leads by points or goals, what does he do in the second half? Plays the harder. If he gets a nasty knock, does he quit? NO, he sticks it. That is the fighting spirit in games. The side with the greater intensity of purpose, the side that sticks reverses, the side that means to *'get there'* wins, must win!.

Games Spirit in War.

It is the same in the game of war. Intensity of purpose, the power to endure, the will to win. The soldier must have the power of endurance, must *'stick it'*, and stick it against reverses, hardships, and sickness. He must fight with the purpose of winning, of getting there and of staying there. That is the fighting spirit in war, the heritage that has come to us through our games. That spirit must imbue all our training, without it, training is artificial and valueless. How did savage tribes, Red Indians, Zulus, Maoris, stimulate and foster the fighting spirit? By war dances – burst of concentrated energy, mental and physical. We must do the same. **We must concentrate our energies upon training with the most savage and aggressive weapon.**

Most Aggressive Weapon.
What is the most aggressive weapon? The weapon of the shortest range! The weapon which compels a man to *'get there'*, to stay there *'the bayonet'*. The training in every weapon is based upon the fighting spirit, the spirit of the shortest range weapon, the *'spirit of the bayonet'*. Men should be made to concentrate regularly upon bayonet training, if only for ten minutes a day. Stir up the fighting spirit in the eager, it will be caught by the others; nothing is so catching or inspiring as enthusiasm. By daily concentration you can easily form a habit. If you want to rise early, what do you do? Before going to sleep you concentrate your thoughts upon rising early, and you wake at the time you wish. If you do this regularly, in a short time you will have formed the habit of rising early. So it is with bayonet training. Concentrate upon it for a few minutes each day, and the *'fighting spirit'* will become part of your nature.

Principles of Training.
There are three principles or *'tips'* which must govern every form of training. They are:-

1. Train with a purpose   2. Train naturally.
3. Train continuously.

Consider the first principle. Men fight as they train. If man trains without a purpose, he will fight without a purpose.
When a man enters a boxing competition, what is his purpose? To knock his opponent out! All his energies are concentrated upon it. If they were not, his training would be purposeless and a sham.

Purpose of War.
What is the purpose of war? *'Killing'*. Every weapon is made for that purpose alone. Every *'Bosche'* killed is a point scored in the killing match. Victory goes to the side which can knock out the other, i.e., which kills most men. Every *'Bosche'* killed brings victory a minute nearer. The purpose of war must be kept always in the mind during training. A soldier is a man who goes into battle wanting to kill and knowing how to kill. The passions which will develop this purpose must be stimulated and he must be trained so that he can carry out this purpose. He must be converted into a *'controlled savage'*. That is the object of the trainer.

Training to be Natural.

To achieve this object the training must be natural. The natural physical and mental atmosphere and the natural material environment of battle must be introduced. Every weapon has its own *'atmosphere'*, just as every weapon has its own uses. The further from the enemy, the more cold-blooded and calculated is the method of destruction; the nearer, the more hot-blooded and savage. The bayonet then is the most *'savage'* of all weapons, because its range is the shortest. This savagery, this *'atmosphere'* of *'seeing red'*, must be brought into the training; but the *'savage'* must be kept under control, must be taught to control himself.

Training for Direction.

Who affords the best example of the controlled savage? The boxer. Let us study and adopt his methods. What does he do? He learns, first, the most vulnerable parts of the body. Then, he practices direction, trains his fist to follow his eye. In bayonet training, then, the first thing a man must learn is where to *'stick'* his opponent; next, never to miss his target. The point of his bayonet must follow the direction of his eye. That is why there is no better shooting practice than pointing at targets with the bayonet – for it trains the eye and strengthens the muscles. What are the appliances necessary to bayonet training? *Ring-sticks, entrenching-tool handles, sacks, sandbags*, anything, in fact, to which may be affixed a disc or target that will show the result of a point.

Training for Strength

To return to the boxer. Having learned direction and the vulnerable spots, what does he do next? Punch, punch, punch; practices punching until he has developed strength, for he knows that in a contest he must punch hard and punch often. What is his fighting kit, and where does he fight? He fights stripped to the waist, practically naked, on a level stage. Under what conditions does a man fight to kill with the *'bayonet'*? He is fully equipped, wears, possibly, a gas-mask. He carries a rifle and bayonet weighing about 13 lbs. He has charged over obstacles and through mud. He fights, perhaps, in a confined space. He has to drive his bayonet home with all his might and to use equal force in withdrawing it. If strength is necessary to the boxer, who fights under almost comfortable conditions, how much more essential is it to the man who fights with the *'bayonet'*, hampered

138

by his equipment, his surroundings, his earlier exertions, and by the weight of the weapon he uses. It is foolish and cruel to send an untrained boxer into the ring; *it is criminal to send a man over unless he is thoroughly trained.*

Bayonet training is simple, simpler than the boxer's. Give a man his daily pointing practice – about 15 minutes a day will do. Unlike the boxer, he needs no fitted gymnasium with elaborate apparatus. He can train anywhere. Bayonet practice strengthens the muscles and steadies the nerve for rifle shooting. Bayonet training and rifle training go '*hand-in-hand*', are interlocked as closely as the rifle and bayonet themselves. Each supplements and helps the other.

Training for Speed.

Good direction is a boxer's first asset, strength his second and speed his third. He must be quick, alert, think quickly, and act quickly. So it is with the man behind the '*bayonet*'. The boxer acquires speed by shadow-fighting, by fighting with the punch-pad and by sparring with his partners. Train a man by the same methods with the bayonet. Let his trainer (his sparring partner) give him quickening practices with the ring-stick (the boxing-pad), and give him '*mad minute*' practices. By these means not only will he acquire skill with his weapon, but his brain will become more alert, more active; this fits him not only for bayonet fighting but for every form of fighting.

Continuity in Training.

Training must be continuous. The more a man is trained, the more skilful he becomes. The more skill he acquires, the more his self-confidence increases. Knowing he can do a thing well, he develops confidence in himself. Knowing his comrades are equally skilful, he gains confidence in them. His confidence is multiplied, for *confidence is at once contagious and inspiring.* What is moral? Moral is confidence in one's self and confidence in one's comrades. It is collective confidence, the spirit of a good boat's crew or football team. Moral can be and must be created. It is begotten by continuous and enthusiastic training.   T h e more a man trains *eye, brain and muscle,* the more readily they work together, until in time they combine spontaneously by reflex action, or what is commonly called second nature. Instances of this can be seen in every match between two good boxers, wherein one responds to the other's feints before the message of the eye can have been more than delivered to the brain. A soldier's brain should be similarly trained, so that in battle it is impelled to do the correct thing naturally, almost automatically, and without conscious effort. This stage is reached, however, only by *careful and continuous training*.

Simplicity in Training.
Training, in order to be continuous, must be simple. The methods of instruction must be simple and little or no apparatus must be needed, so that training may be carried on anywhere and by anybody. Training which can be carried out solely by highly-trained specialists is doomed in war-time. *Training which requires quantities of elaborate apparatus is also doomed.* Training which can be carried out only in water-tight compartments and cannot be combined with its kindred branches of training is unnatural and signs its own *death-warrant*. Bayonet-training suffers from none of these defects. It can be directed by platoon or section commanders. It can be carried out, if necessary, without any form of special equipment, on any ground and in bad weather even in billets and confined spaces.

Inter-Dependability of Weapons.
Success in battle depends upon *mutual support*, upon how much and how well one type of weapon helps the others. It must be the same in training. The exponents of one branch of training must work in concert with and assist the exponents of other branches, and must not, under any circumstances, disparage them or oppose them. In training a football team, would you have one trainer for the forwards, another for the halves and another for the backs? No. Although each type of player has a different role to sustain, it is the development of the team as a whole that is desired, *collectivism,* pulling together, for the team whose forwards disparaged its halves, or whose halves 'let down' its backs, would have but a sorry chance of success. To secure good combination, the footballers train together as a team; and *so must the various training branches of the army*.

The Team of Weapons.
Every soldier has to know how to use at least four weapons. They are the team of which he is certain and which he must handle and direct. What are the weapons? *Bayonet, bullet, bomb and entrenching-tool.* They are the team he captains. The soldier has

always handled this team from the very earliest days, for the weapons of war have changed only in form, not in principle, and *the principles of fighting have never changed and never will.* Go back to the Battle of Crecy. What was the rifle then? The box. The *bayonet?* The *pike spear or axe.* The *bullet?* The *arrow.* The entrenching tool? The shield! for instead of digging his cover the soldier carried it upon his arm.

Team versus Specialist.

An early example of the triumph of team work over specialization in one particular branch is seen in the Biblical story of the fight between '*David and Goliath*'. Goliath, the giant, was a specialist in the use of the sword. Heavily armored, protected by a shield and wielding a heavy sword, he was almost immobile, a veritable '*strong point*'. David, had he listened to his advisors, would have become another strong point. But he would have none of their Armour. He was a tactician. He recognized the value of mobility. He recognized, too, the value of team work. He took a rifle – his sling, and ammunition – pebbles from the brook. Then he advanced to the attack. He opened fire – fire application – on Goliath, and put a barrage on the '*strong point*'. The fire demoralized the giant. The pebble struck him on the forehead. He fell. David realized that it was time for the next member of the team – *the bayonet* – to get to work. He jumped in, grabbed the giant's sword and finished with the bayonet the work which the bullet had begun.

Unchanging Principles.

It is the same to-day. '*Bullet and bayonet*'. The tools have evolved, but the principle is unchanged. David got to close quarters and finished with the sword the work the pebble had begun at long range. He was the better natural fighter. When the tactical application of the bayonet – *assault training* – is being carried out, don't concentrate solely on the bayonet. Develop good team work. Train the men in the worldly principles of fighting. Keep the picture of the battle always in your min's eye.

The Advance.

Before you advance, look before you leap. In London you are told to '*look round*' before you step off the pavement. How much more necessary is it then to '*look round*' before you step over the parapet. Before going '*over the top*' study the ground over which the assault is to be made. How do you do this? By patrolling the ground at night. Let your men know you have done this. By studying maps and airplane photos. Don't make a reckless charge over unknown ground. By doing so you would be courting failure and would throw away valuable lives to no good purpose. *Remember always look before you leap.*

Necessity of Protection.

When you do leap – advance, you need something more than a thorough knowledge of your ground. What is it? *Protection.* Never advance except under some form of cover or protection. There are many forms of cover. Artificial cover: The fire of artillery, machine-gun or rifle – mutual support. Natural cover: Folds of the ground, woods, buildings etc. Atmospheric cover, or cover of the elements: *Darkness, mist, fog, rain, snow.* Then there is the cover of surprise (*The most effective cover*). Men must be taught to utilize every form of cover during assault training. To do so they must be kept well in hand, well under control, especially when advancing with the intention to kill with the bayonet, for, although they 'see red' and have become savages, they must, like the boxer, be 'controlled savages'. If men are well under control they are ready for any emergency, to dig-in, to open fire or to charge.

Charging Distance.

What is the ideal assaulting distance? Remember the great maxim of the Bayonet, *'To kill with the bayonet meet a man harder than he meets you'*. Never, therefore, charge more than 20 yards, but charge then as though you were running for a long jump – increase your pace as you near the objective, the enemy. Suppose an assault to have been successful, the line has reached its objective and cleared it with the bayonet. What happens next? The enemy has the position registered and down comes his barrage. Which member of the team takes up the game? *The entrenching-tool (the shield of olden days).*

The Counter-Attack.

What is likely to happen next? A counter-attack. What comes into play? The bullet. A man must be trained to stay in the trench and fire so long as a round of ammunition is left to him. The bullet travels a thousand times farther and a thousand times faster than the bayonet. It is easier to apply, and *one bullet may by good luck kill two or three of the enemy.* But men must not fire wildly. Up to now they have been making an intense physical effort; now they must make an intense mental effort – control. To smash a counter-attack, destroy first the experts who control and support it. Shoot down the machine-gunners, who may be supporting from either flank; concentrate upon the officers and NCOs. And, finally, settle with the rank and file. The best method of controlling excited men is to get them to aim at definite targets, to select their victims and to select them with judgment.

Cleaning-Up.

After the *'counter-attack'* is broken, there may still remain, in trenches and holes near by, lurking enemies who may give infinite trouble. You cannot see them, so it is of no use shooting. It is wasting lives to send men at them with the *'bayonet'*. How will you deal with them? Bring the last member of the team into the game, *the bomb.* So there you have it (*Rifle, bayonet, entrenching-tool, and bomb*). Every member of the team knows his role and plays his part. But *'counter-attacs'* do not invariably find you waiting ready with a store of ammunition. It may be entirely exhausted. How then will you act when the counter attack develops?

A Picture from Life.

A picture from life is worth all the theory in the world. How did the 52nd Australian Infantry act under circumstances similar to those propounded above? Two companies were holding trenches that had been heavily bombarded. But the men had used their entrenching tools well and, although out of ammunition, were still holding on. Then the *'Bosche'* developed his *'counter-attack'*, with two companies, advancing in four waves from a distance of about 400 yards.

Waiting.

Should the Australians have rushed out to meet them halfway? No, they should not, and they did not. They did the right thing. They let the *'Bosche'* lines advance, for the farther they traveled the more tired and disorganized the men would become, and the artillery and machine-gunners in rear would get a change to range on them. When the leading line was about 100 yards away, the Australians got out of their trenches. *In front or behind?* In Front, for had they got out behind, the trenches would have checked the impetus of their counter-charge. They got out front and waited. When waiting for an assault, should a man look upon the whole advancing line? No, for as surely as he does, he will imagine that the whole line is advancing upon him and upon him alone! He should select a *'victim'* and concentrate all his gaze and intention upon him. This is what the Australians did.

Advancing.

When the first *'Bosche'* line was about 60 yards away, the Australians advanced at a jog trot, with *their rifles carried at the high port*. There are two reasons for carrying the rifle at the high port. First, it is a signal for the assault, and, secondly, the bolt and muzzle are thereby well off the ground, clear of mud and mud splashes.

Counter-Charging.

When the lines were about 20 yards apart the Australians charged. Napoleon has said that two lines charging with the bayonet will never meet, because the line which charges with the greatest fury will demoralize the other. That was certainly true in this case. The *'Bosche'* did not wait. His first line bolted. Should the Australian s have chased them? No, for they would have screened the fire of any artillery or machine guns behind them which might have ranged upon the *fleeing Germans*. The Australians lie down and let shell and bullet finish the work which the *'spirit of the bayonet'* had begun. This was one of the best conceived and best executed pieces of work of that *stage of the war*. Practically two whole battalions of *Prussian Guards* were wiped out. That is a good example of team work. Bayonet did not actually score many points – kill many *'Bosche'*, but that was not his job. Bullet and shall are the scorers. Bayonet supplies the spirit essential to every assault.

The Bayonet Spirit.

The *psychological value* of the bayonet is not always realized. It is not always given credit for the part it plays, because, like the work of Rugby forward, its share in the game is not directly obvious. It may be objected that men have been in five or six assaults and yet have never had occasion or opportunity to use the *'bayonet'*. What, therefore, it is asked, is the use of bayonet training? But, what makes a man ready and eager to go forward with bayonet? Confidence in and familiarity with the weapon.

Eager to *'get there'* and use it. What makes the *'Bosche'* throw up his hands when he sees the bayonet? *The consciousness that the Britisher is a better natural fighter,* a better bayonet fighter, than himself. He has admitted the fact openly. Don't let us reverse the positions by neglecting bayonet training. The *'bayonet'* is the *'soul of an attack'* but, in carrying out assault training, always include with the bayonet the bullet, the entrenching tool and the bomb. *Be large-minded and make your training natural.*

Army's Greatest Force.

What is the greatest force in an army? *The private soldier.* Get the private soldier to train himself. You will then solve nine-tenths of the problems of training and vitalize the entire army. Get him to realize that he is a member of a great team that the success of the team depends upon each man *'playing the game'* and doing something for his side. He will appreciate the situation. Nearly every Britisher has *'played the game'* at football and can be induced to do the same in military training. What made our British bowmen such wonderful fighters? Voluntary training and constant practice on the village green. Create the *voluntary spirit,* the spirit of individual effort, and you will kindle throughout the army a flame which cannot be extinguished, *a spirit which is indomitable.*

Self-Training.

A man fights as he trains. If he trains *'on his own'*, he will fight on his own, when he has neither leaders nor comrades. Bayonet training is so simple that any two men can one another. How do you induce men to train and get fit for boxing? *By holding frequent competitions.* Do the same for the bayonet and you will get similar results? There are many forms of simple bayonet competition, which can be carried out anywhere and which require no elaborate apparatus or equipment. Organize these competitions, arouse the competitive spirit of the men, catch their interest and you will have no difficulty in getting them to train *'on their own'*. Remember if you want your men to make an effort the effort must first come from their leaders – their officers and NCOs.

Value of Voluntary Training.

When you have awakened this *enthusiasm* you will have accomplished a *triumph.* Ten minutes of voluntary training during leisure hours are worth ten hours of compulsory training during working days. The value of training lies not in the amount done, but rather in the spirit in which it is done. *Spirit is catching.* The spirit of one man will spread to a crowd, to an army, to a nation. The spirit created in one branch of training will spread to another. The *'spirit of the bayonet'* will spread, is spreading, throughout the entire army. An army fights as it trains, and our army has fought, is fighting, and will fight in the go forward *'get there'* spirit of its training.

1. An example of many postcards sent by member of the Army Gymnastic Staff during the First World War. (Reproduced courtesy of the Royal Army Physical Training Corps Museum)

"EACH DUMMY MUST BE REGARDED AS AN ACTUAL ARMED OPPONENT."

Para. 55, Sec. V,
"Bayonet Training"
(Reprint, 1916).

2. A postcard that was used to emphasise particular instructions from the *Bayonet Training Manual*, 1916. (Reproduced courtesy of the Royal Army Physical Training Corps Museum).

3. Assault training with fixed bayonets outside the Headquarters Gymnasium, Aldershot, 1916.

4. A bayonet fighting demonstration with an improvised pugil stick and hook to instruct in the use of a bayonet in close-quarters combat, c. 1916. (Reproduced courtesy of the Royal Army Physical Training Corps Museum)

5. Bayonet practice carried out in a mock trench outside the Headquarters Gymnasium, Aldershot, under the supervision of an Army Gymnastic Staff instructor, 1916. (Reproduced courtesy of the Royal Army Physical Training Corps Museum)

6. Physical Training activities conducted outside the Headquarters Gymnasium, Aldershot, *c.* 1900, on what is now the Army Athletics track. (Reproduced courtesy of the Royal Army Physical Training Corps Museum)

7. A view from inside the Headquarters Gymnasium, Aldershot, *c.* 1900. (Reproduced courtesy of the Royal Army Physical Training Corps Museum)

6

Methods of Unarmed Attack and Defence, 1917

No man's land, the area between the opposing trenches, consisting of a shell-pocketed waste land and heavily spiked barbed wire, was the area of operation for raiding parties of both sides. Savage hand-to-hand fighting accompanied artillery and machine-gun fire and, without adequate training for such circumstances, the chances of survival were minimal.

Training for special raiding parties was often carried out under the supervision of Major R. B. Campbell and his instructors. Campbell himself was meticulous in his preparation and acknowledged as an expert in trench raiding. Before any raid took place, Campbell would have the enemy trenches photographed and reconstructed so the exact layout and terrain could be used for training. Although his role was to train troops, Campbell was famous for going over the top with junior officers during offensives, dictating notes to his subordinate as to what he observed as the events unfolded. On returning, he and his instructors would review his notes, enabling them to work out methods of dealing with situations he had actually witnessed.

Campbell, a former Army boxing champion, did not work alone in devising methods of unarmed defence against the bayonet, knife, club, rifle butt and sword. He surrounded himself with Army Gymnastic instructors who were champions in their own right: Billy Wells, Jimmy Driscoll and Jimmy Wilde were all boxing champions and arguably all-time greats. When British raiding parties returned from German trenches with boxes of spiked knuckledusters and maces, they were sent straight to Campbell so he and his instructors could determine the best method of unarmed counter-attack.[1]

Wrestling was also recognised as adding invaluable benefit in the grim hand-to-hand struggles that accompanied nightly raids. Wrestling was systematically taught and practiced by the British

Army under the supervision of Army Gymnastic Staff instructors in gymnasia across Britain, as well as schools of instruction and convalescent camps in France. Wrestling, in relation to unarmed combat, had a definite military value as it was competitive and, like boxing, could be used to foster team spirit. As a form physical training it required agility, endurance and quick judgment. It provided the British soldier with a natural method of overcoming attack from behind by utilising the enemy's own aggression and showed them how best to use their weight to conserve their strength when in the clutches of the enemy.[2]

The following reproduction of the Method of Unarmed Attack and Defence pamphlet, produced in 1917, provides examples of the techniques devised by Campbell and his staff for soldiers carrying out unarmed combat. This pamphlet would later become the 'Unarmed Fighting' chapter of the 1918 *Physical Training Manual*, which included physical training tables and games.

40
W.O.
4195

METHODS OF UNARMED ATTACK AND DEFENCE.

PART   I.—Simple methods of unarmed attack and defence, &c., which can be taught to all recruits.

PART   II.—More advanced methods for trained soldiers, &c.

PART III.—Special methods for military police, &c.

(Issued by the General Staff, June, 1917.)

LONDON:
PRINTED FOR HIS MAJESTY'S STATIONERY OFFICE,
BY HARRISON & SONS, 45-47, ST. MARTIN'S LANE, W.C. 2.

1917.

PART I.

Simple methods of unarmed attack and defence, &c., which can be taught to all recruits.

ATTACK (BOTH UNARMED).

1. (Fig. 1).—Attack with a direct kick, bringing the foot back at once, to avoid it being caught by opponent.

If opponent is standing left foot forward, kick with the left foot, and *vice versa.*

Points to attack : Knee, fork, stomach and head, according to position.

A kick at the knee is the least easily countered, and is best.

2. When fighting an opponent facing you at close quarters, seize him behind the shoulders with both hands, and pull him swiftly towards you; then proceed as in Fig. 2, or in any other way which will rapidly place your opponent *hors de combat.*

3. Place corresponding leg, viz., left to left, behind your opponent's, kick backwards at his heel to force it forward ; at the same time push his face away from you.

4. (Fig. 3).—When behind your opponent, seize his shoulders at the full extent of both arms, and pull him swiftly towards you, at the same time kicking the back of his knee with the hollow of your foot.

5. If, when struggling with an opponent, you should both fall down, drive one of your elbows into his stomach or sharply against his chin.

DEFENCE AND COUNTER-ATTACK (BOTH UNARMED).

6. *Opponent grips throat with both hands from in front.*—Swing your right arm up and over opponent's wrists, at the same time vigorously turning the body on the hips.

When opponent's hold is broken, cut at his jugular vein with the edge of the right hand, keeping the fingers outstretched and rigid.

7. (*Same Attack.*)—(Fig. 4 (*a*).) Seize and push opponent's wrists outwards (Fig. 4 (*b*)) gripping his right wrist with your right hand. The moment his hold is broken (Fig. 4 (*c*)) grip his right arm from the back above the elbow with your left hand; if you then push with both hands, he is at your mercy.

8. *When seized by an opponent from behind.*—(Fig. 5.) Throw your head violently backwards, in an endeavour to hit him in the face.

9. (Fig. 6.) If unsuccessful in this, bend rapidly down with your legs astride, and endeavour to seize one of his legs and pull it violently upwards.

10. If opponent grips you round the arms and above the elbows, trap his arms, stoop swiftly forward and throw him over your head.

11. If you cannot succeed with these counter-attacks, seize one of his fingers and break it back; this will make him release his grip, when you can attack him.

12. *Standing Armlock.*—If opponent strikes at your face (Fig. 7), grip his wrist with both hands, turn quickly inwards, placing your back to opponent; at the same time pull his arm, palm upwards, as far as possible over your shoulder, and pull downwards.

13. If, during a struggle, you should fall down and your opponent remain standing, lie on your back and parry his attacks with your legs.

METHODS OF CARRYING WOUNDED.

14. *Standing up.*—(Fig. 8 (*a*).) Stand facing the wounded man, grasp his right wrist with your left hand; (Fig. 8 (*b*)) put your right upper arm under his fork and lift him on to your shoulders.

15. *Lying down.*—Turn the wounded man on to his back (Fig. 9 (*a*)), kneel down on your inside knee, and raise him to a sitting position and then as high as possible; (Fig. 9 (*b*)) grasp his right wrist with your left hand, put your head under his right armpit; (Fig. 9 (*c*)) feel for the balance and lift; then put your right arm under his fork.

PART II.

More advanced methods for trained soldiers, &c.

ATTACK (BOTH UNARMED).

1. *Cross Buttock*—(Fig. 10.) Force your buttock into the small of opponent's back, and overbalance him with a strong swing of your arm round his throat.

If opponent's right foot is forward, the right buttock and right arm should be used, and *vice versa.*

2. *When attacked by an opponent who tries to kick.*— (Fig. 11.) Turn sideways and hop towards him on your rear foot, the front leg being raised and bent at an angle to act as a parry and to protect your vulnerable parts.

If he kicks with his right leg, turn your left side towards him, and *vice versa.*

When you have closed with him, act as in Part II, 1.

3. *When seized from behind with one or both hands.*— Wrench off opponent's hand by seizing his thumb and pressing it backwards, and pull his arm over your corresponding shoulder.

By turning the palm upwards, he is secured with the " standing armlock " (I, 12).

By turning the palm downwards, he can be thrown with the ' flying mare " (III, 3).

DEFENCE AND COUNTER-ATTACK.

4. *Leglock.*—As your opponent kicks at you, turn quickly sideways and parry with the fleshy part of your front leg. (Fig. 12 (*a*).) Seize opponent's leg as he kicks, and gripping his foot turn it sharply inwards; (Fig. 12 (*b*)) this will cause him to fall down; (Fig. 12 (*c*)) maintain your hold on his foot, and push the leg you are holding across his other leg, which must then be forced up and over the shin, thus securing a leglock.

5. *Seized from the front with both hands.*—Smartly grasp belt or clothing in the region of opponent's waist with one hand, and pull him smartly towards you; as you pull with one hand, push the other against his face. The combined push and pull will throw him down.

6. *Seized from the front with one hand.*—Grip the wrist of the offending hand with your opposite hand; put free hand to opponent's face and push.

7. *To march a prisoner back to the lines.*—(Fig. 13.) Take his right wrist with your right hand, put your left arm over his right upper arm, bend your elbow and bring your left forearm back under his right forearm. Press down with your right hand and up with your left forearm.

His right palm should be uppermost.

8. *Armlock.*—Grasp opponent's right wrist with your right hand, and turn his palm uppermost, thrust your left arm under his upper arm and grasp his clothing near the neck. Press down with your right hand and up with your left arm.

UNARMED DEFENCE AGAINST ATTACK WITH DAGGER.

9. *High.*—(Fig. 14 (*a*).) Parry with the opposite arm to that with which opponent attacks; *i.e.*, if he attacks with his right, parry with your left; (Fig. 14 (*b*)) thrust

your right arm beneath his outstretched arm, upper arm against upper arm, double his arm back from the elbow with your left hand and seize his wrist with your right hand. Pull it down, using the upper arm as a lever; (Fig. 14 (c)) now bend his fist inwards with your left hand until his fingers open and he drops his weapon.

10. *Low.*—(Fig. 15 (a).) Parry in a similar way, with the forearm bent across the stomach; (Fig. 15 (b)) the forearm should always meet the opponent's wrist; (Fig. 15 (c)) quickly turn your back to opponent, whilst swinging your opposite arm over his, and apply " standing armlock " (I, 12).

UNARMED DEFENCE AGAINST ATTACK WITH RIFLE AND BAYONET.

11. (Fig. 16 (a).) As opponent makes his " point " fend it off with the right hand; (Fig. 16 (b)) step forward and seize his left hand with both yours, the left under his palm, the right over his fingers, and give a sharp twist outwards.

12. (Fig. 17 (a).) As opponent makes his " point " parry it outwards with the left hand, and (Fig. 17 (b)) stepping in seize opponent's left wrist firmly with the right hand; (Fig. 17 (c)) grasp the rifle just below the bayonet with the left hand, back of the hand down, and (Fig. 17 (d)) swing it violently upwards and over to the right, at the same time stepping in and kicking, or bringing the left knee into the lower part of the opponent's body.

13. As opponent makes his " point " parry it outwards with the right hand, and stepping in kick at lower part of body or shin. (Fig. 18 (a).) Grasp the rifle just below the bayonet with the right hand, back of the hand down, (Fig. 18 (b)) and swing it upwards and over to the left; (Fig. 18 (c)) force the point of the bayonet to the ground, and stepping in (Fig. 18 (d)) either charge opponent down or trip him.

PART III.

Special methods for military police, &c.

1. *Headlock.*—When opponent is holding with both hands on to some fixed object, swing one arm round his neck, push your buttocks into his, and pull him away.

2. *Crutch hold from a " punch."*—Grip the wrist of your opponent's outstretched arm, and place your other arm between his legs; this will bring your head under his outstretched arm.

Lift him off the ground and throw him over your head.

3. *Flying mare.*—(Fig. 19 (*a*).) Grasp opponent's wrist, turn inwards quickly, getting your shoulder well under his armpit; (Fig. 19 (*b*)) pull his arm over your shoulder, and, stooping smartly forward, fling him to the ground.

Fig. 1.

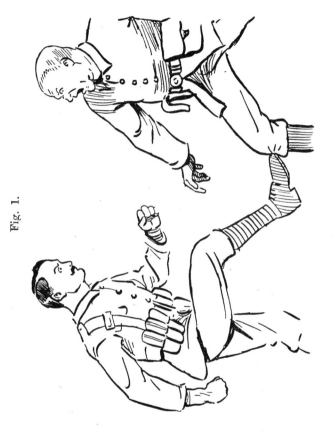

Fig. 2.

Fig. 3.

A 3

Fig. 4 (a).

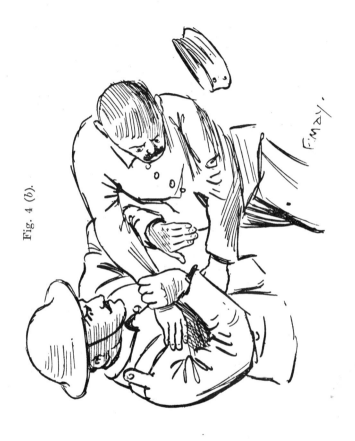

Fig. 4 (b).

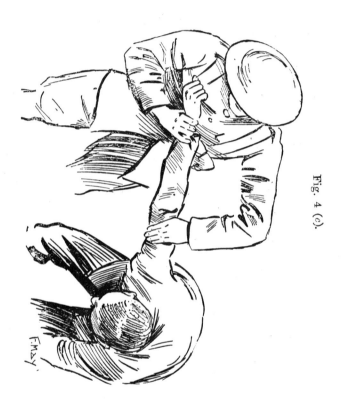

Fig. 4 (c).

Fig. 5.

Fig. 6.

F. May

Fig. **7.**

Fig. 8 (*a*).

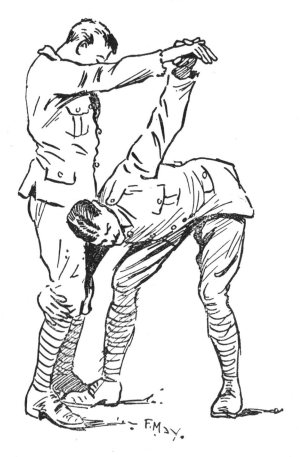

Fig. 8 (b).

Fig. 9 (a).

Fig. 9 (b).

Fig. 9 (c).

Fig. 10.

Fig. 11.

Fig. 12 (a).

Fig. 12 (b).

Fig. 12 (c).

Fig. 13.

FMay

Fig. 14 (a).

Fig. 14 (b).

Fig. 14 (c).

Fig. 15 (a).

Fig. 15 (b).

Fig. 15 (c).

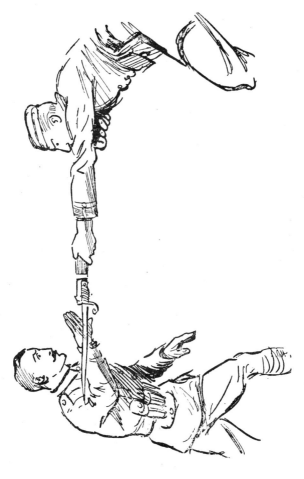

Fig. 16 (a).

Fig. 16 (b).

Fig. 17 (a).

Fig. 17 (b).

Fig. 17 (c).

Fig. 17 (d).

Fig. 18 (a).

Fig. 18 (b).

Fig. 18 (c).

Fig. 18 (d).

Fig. 19 (a).

Fig. 19 (b).

F. S. Moy

7

Recreational Training and Games

In December 1916, a scheme of recreational training for soldiers was launched by Second-Lieutenant F. J. Starr, who was appointed as the Recreational Training Officer.[1] Starr was more than a sports enthusiast; he had once been a sports journalist who wrote a weekly column called 'Service Gossip' in the *Athletic News*,[2] and was a strong believer that the use of games in physical training would, as bayonet instruction did, help to improve fitness and build morale. Games and recreational training provided men returning from the trenches with an existence that resembled normality and aided in preventing mental exhaustion. Recreational activities included football, boxing, cross-country, athletics, baseball, wrestling and assault training. Games and recreational activities utilised the same exercises that were found in the training tables, but the variety of these activities helped to alleviate the monotony of carrying out physical training and service life in general.

At the same time that the scheme for recreational training was launched, a conference for superintendents of Physical and Bayonet Training took place. It was decided at this conference that no money prizes would be awarded for recreational training or competition in the British Expeditionary Force. This decision would be officially confirmed by General Routine Order, but initially only applied to boxing. It would not be until 1918 that the recreational training pamphlet reproduced here ensured that the regulation would apply to all athletic activities.[3] The issue of no money prizes was controversial, so much so that nine out of ten officers believed that soldiers would not box for any other kind of prize. Fortunately this was not the case, and boxers often surprised themselves by wishing to receive a medal or other memento for winning their contest.[4] Examples of the registered recreational training medals and cups that were available to troops for the various sports and games are located at the end of the pamphlet.

When the responsibility for conducting bayonet training was transferred to the Musketry Staff, the Physical and Bayonet Training Staff replaced the 'Bayonet' in their title for 'Recreational'. The following year, the Physical and Recreational Training Staff would become the Army Physical Training Staff, a title which would be retained until it received its 'corps' status on 16 September 1940. The British Expeditionary Forces Sports Board was formed in early 1919, and its success was owed to the pioneering work done by the men of the Army Physical Training Staff. It became responsible for the administration of sports in the British Army.[5]

Games for Use with Physical Training Tables and Training in Bombing, which was first distributed in October 1916, would provide physical training instructors with additional means of conducting daily physical training tables while preventing monotony. Games such as 'Bomb Ball' had the additional benefit of providing specific physical conditioning for an actual military task – the quick and accurate throwing of a grenade. A 'Games' section would be included in supplementary physical training tables from 1917, as well as in the Physical Training pamphlet printed in 1918.

(Issued with Army Orders dated 1st October, 1916.)

40/W.O./3263

GAMES

FOR USE WITH

PHYSICAL TRAINING TABLES AND TRAINING IN BOMBING.

1916.

LONDON:
PRINTED UNDER THE AUTHORITY OF HIS MAJESTY'S STATIONERY OFFICE,
BY HARRISON AND SONS, 45–47, ST. MARTIN'S LANE, W.C.
PRINTERS IN ORDINARY TO HIS MAJESTY.

GAMES

For use with Physical Training Tables and Training in Bombing.

GENERAL REMARKS.

The essence of the following games is that they should be conducted with the utmost amount of energy and the rigid observance of all the details connected with them.

Executed in this way, they inculcate discipline and develop quickness of brain and movement, whereas, if carelessly carried out, they may do more harm than good.

A game may be introduced into the daily P.T. Table to prevent monotony, either before or after the Marching and Jumping Exercises or in place of them, according to the time available.

Games should not be continued for too long, and must not be carried out to the detriment of P.T. proper. Maximum time devoted to games during a Table should never exceed 10 minutes.

INDEX.

1. JUMPING THE BAG.

Formation.—The players stand in a circle at close intervals and facing inward.

Apparatus.—A light rope 5 to 8 yards long, to one end of which is attached a small bag of canvas or leather filled with sand and weighing about 1 lb,

Method of Playing.—The Instructor stands in the centre of the ring and swings the bag round, gradually paying out the rope until it becomes necessary for the players to jump to avoid it. The direction in which the bag is swung should be varied. The rate of swinging as well as height of the bag from the ground should be gradually increased. The object of the players is, of course, to avoid being caught by the rope or bag and brought to the ground.

Common Faults.

Some of the players stand outside the ring, the bag thus not passing under their feet.

2. SIMPLE RELAY RACE.

(*a*) **Formation.**—Two parallel lines are marked out about 20 to 50 yards apart.

Each team is divided into two parts containing an equal number of players.

These are drawn up on the parallel lines, facing one another and extended at intervals of about **1** yard.

Method of Playing.—On the word " Go," the left hand man of each team drawn up on the one line, races to and touches the outstretched hand of the man immediately opposite him. As soon as his hand has been touched, the latter races similarly to the next man opposite, and so on, the team whose last man first crosses the line being the winners.

(*b*) **Progression.**—Instead of touching a partner, a stick or other article may be carried and transferred, not thrown, from man to man.

Common Faults.

(1) Not waiting to be touched by a partner, or not waiting to receive the stick, &c., before starting.

(2) Standing in front of, instead of " toeing," the line.

3. THREE DEEP.

(*a*) **Formation.**—Players pair. One pair will be told off as " Chaser" and " Runner." Remaining pairs form a double ring, one man standing behind the other, with at least 2 yards between pairs who face the centre of the ring.

Method of Playing.—"Chaser" and "Runner" take up their positions just outside the ring at opposite points of it. On the word "Go," the "Chaser" pursues the "Runner" with the object of "touching" him. If he succeeds, "Chaser" becomes "Runner," and *vice versâ*. "Runner" can take refuge by placing himself, facing inwards, in front of a pair, whereupon the rear man of this pair, now three deep, immediately takes up the rôle of "Runner."

(b) Progression.

Formation.—As above, except that the men of each pair face one another about one yard apart.

Method of Playing.—As above, except that the "Runner" takes refuge *between* a pair, when the one to whom he turns his back becomes "Runner," and the late "Runner" steps back into his place.

This form of the game requires continual alertness on the part of both men in each pair.

Common Faults.

(1) The "Runner" dodges about too long before taking refuge, thus making the game tedious for the others.

(2) In (a) the "Chaser" and "Runner" dodge between the two men forming a pair. This is often due to the outer man not standing close enough to the inner one.

(3) The ring is allowed to grow too small. This is bound to occur unless each pair is careful to step back a short pace to its proper relative position in the ring every time a " Runner " halts in front of it.

4. "UNDER PASSING " RELAY RACE.

Apparatus.—Two or more objects about the size of a croquet ball, *i.e.*, balls made out of rags or paper, boxing gloves, &c.

Formation.—Players are formed into two or more ranks (according to numbers of men and balls available), facing the flank.

Method of Playing.—All the players, excepting the last one of each row, stand with their feet at least 3 foot-lengths apart, bend forward from the hips and grasp the hips or belt of the man in front.

The leading player of each row holds the ball ; the rear one bends down in a position of readiness to receive it.

At the word " Go," the leading man throws the ball, or other object, backwards to the rear man, between his own legs and those of the other players of his row. The ball should be thrown so as to skim the ground. Should it not reach the rear man in one throw, the nearest player must seize it and pass it on in the same way. As soon as the rear man receives it, he must run to the front of his row and go through the same procedure as No. 1, and so on until the last man gets it, *i.e.*, the original leader. The latter races to the front and places the ball on the ground in front of his feet ; the first rank to do this is declared the winner.

Should the ball go outside the players' legs, the player at that spot must fetch it, return to his place and pass it on as described.

Common Faults.

The ball is thrown to the side or too high, instead of straight and skimming the ground.

5. "PLACING THE INDIAN CLUB" RELAY RACE.

(*a*) **Apparatus.**—Two or more Indian Clubs or some similar objects.

Formation.—As in "Under Passing" Relay Race. Opposite, and at about 15 and 20 yards respectively from the front man of each row, two circles of about 8 inches diameter are marked on the ground, one straight behind the other. In the nearest of each of the circles an Indian Club or other object is placed standing on end.

Method of Playing.—At the word "Go," the first player of each row races to the first circle, seizes the club with the left (right) hand, and with the same hand stands it up in the second circle situated 5 yards off. He then races back and touches the outstretched hand of the next man of his row. The latter then races to the club and in the same way places it back in the near circle, and so on alternately until each man of the row has had his turn. The last man, having deposited the club in the circle, races back to the line which the front men were originally "toeing." The first row to finish are of course the winners. Each man, after having touched the outstretched hand of the "next to run," places himself at the rear of his row, which keeps moving forward so that the "next to run" is always "toeing" the original line.

Should the club fall over, the player responsible must replace it in position before the game may be continued.

(*b*) **Progression.**—Between the front man and the nearest circle of each row (which distances should be increased in this case to almost double) a circle of about 1 to 2 yards diameter is drawn.

Each player must, on his way to the club, run round this circle from left to right, and on his way back from right to left. Procedure otherwise as already described.

Common Faults.

(1) Using both hands or the wrong one to place the club,

(2) Players overstepping the line before being touched by the returning man.

(3) Running round the circles in the wrong direction.

6. "WHIP TO THE GAP."

Apparatus.—A knotted handkerchief, towel or other suitable object.

Formation.—The players stand in a ring at close intervals, lean forward, look on the ground in front of them, and hold their hands behind their backs.

Method of Playing.—The Instructor walks or runs round the outside of the ring and as secretly as possible places the handkerchief in the hands of one of the players. The latter at once chases his right (left) hand neighbour, beating him with the handkerchief as he runs round the ring back to his place.

Both then take their places in the ring and the Instructor proceeds again as before.

The latter should endeavour to deceive the players as much as possible as to whom the handkerchief has been given.

Common Faults.

Players looking round to see who receives the handkerchief.

7. CHANGING PLACES.

Formation.—All the players but one stand in a circle of about 7 yards or more diameter, facing inward. The odd player stands in the middle.

Method of Playing.—Each player is given a number, which he retains all through the game. The Instructor calls out two numbers (but not, of course, that of the player in the middle), and the players so numbered must change places in the circle. While they are doing so the odd player must try to get into one of the vacated places first, and if he is successful the ousted player then becomes the odd man in the centre.

8. CIRCLE TOUCH BALL.

Apparatus.—A football.

Formation.—Players stand in a circle 1 to 2 paces apart, facing inward, with one player inside the circle.

Method of Playing.—The football is passed, by hand, from one player to another, and the player inside the circle endeavours to intercept it. If successful, he changes places with the last thrower. If the ball falls to the ground, the player responsible either for the bad pass or missed catch—at the discretion of the Instructor— changes places with the player inside the circle.

Common Faults.

(1) The ball is held too long before passing (about 3 seconds may be put as a time limit for holding the ball).

(2) The ball is kicked, which is wrong, and spoils the whole idea of the game.

9. MAZE.

Formation.—All the players, except two, stand in parallel ranks one behind the other. The distance between each player and each rank is that of "double arm's length," so that whichever direction the ranks may face with arms extended horizontally a line of players with finger tips touching will be formed. The ranks should be drawn up so as to form a square as nearly as possible.

Method of Playing.—The chaser has to pursue the runner up and down the lines until he catches him, neither being permitted to pass under the outstretched arms. The Instructor makes sudden changes in the lines by calling out "Right turn" or "Left turn," on which all turn in the required direction, still keeping the arms outstretched. These sudden changes alter the direction of the paths down which the two players may run. The interest depends greatly upon the judgment of the Instructor in giving the commands "Right (or Left) turn." They should be given frequently and sharply, and often just at the moment when the chaser is about to catch the runner.

The game continues until the runner is caught or a time limit reached, when a new chaser and runner are selected.

Common Faults.

(1) Chaser or runner passing under outstretched arms.

(2) Not changing the chaser and runner sufficiently often.

10. BOMB-BALL.

A game for bringing into play the muscles used in bombing, and for the development of quick and accurate throwing.

Ground.—Any football ground or open space, marked out as under ; the size of the rectangle may be varied to suit the amount of ground available.

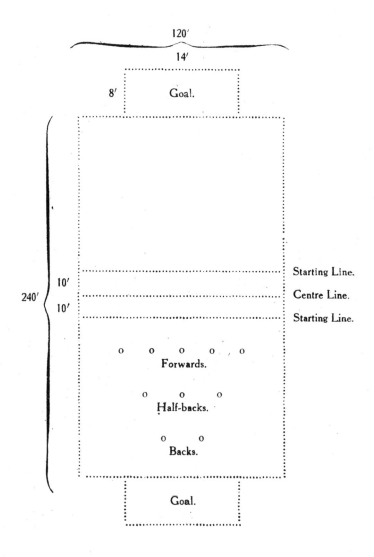

The goal should be marked out on the ground, no goal-posts being necessary.

Teams.—The players should be disposed as in Association Football, but a lesser number than eleven a side should take part if the ground be small.

Apparatus.—Some object approximating to the weight, size and shape of a grenade, care being taken that it is not such as to be likely to injure the players. The following is suggested :—a small oval-shaped bag of canvas or thick calico, filled with sand or small shot to the required weight and securely sewn up.

Referee.—A referee should control the game, as in football.

Method of Playing.—The ball is passed from player to player by hand, the object being to land it in the goal. It may be passed backward or forward as in Association Football, and the "off-side" rule will apply in the same way. The passes are taken on the run, and the ball must not be held but passed on immediately. If dropped, the ball must be picked up and similarly passed on at once.

The ball may be caught with both hands, but must only be thrown by one. Only two methods of throwing are allowed : (1) For long distances, a full over-hand throw, as shown in the diagrams in " Training and

Employment of Bombers," March, 1916 ; (2) For short distances, a " put," made in the same manner as " putting-the-shot."

In order to exercise equally both sides of the body and to develop skill and accuracy with both hands, the throwing-hand may be changed every 10 minutes or so, ât the discretion of the Referee.

To start the game, Captains toss, and the winner has the first throw and the right to select the goal he wishes to defend. The teams are then drawn up, the forwards along their respective starting-lines. The referee blows his whistle and the game commences by the centre-forward taking the first throw or " put."

In the course of the game, if the ball lands in the goal, or is caught in the goal and subsequently dropped within it by any player, a goal is scored.

If the ball is caught in the goal before touching the ground and thrown out at once no goal is scored.

If the ball goes "behind" or into "touch," it is thrown in similarly as in Association Football, but with one hand, and this also applies to a " corner."

After a goal has been scored, the game is started again as at the commencement.

Charging.—No charging or rough play is admissible. Passes may be intercepted, or throws frustrated, with the open hand.

Fouls.—Fouls may be given for (1) Running with the ball, instead of passing it at once as soon as caught or picked up ; (2) Throwing the ball in any way but the two methods allowed ; (3) Catching hold of a player ; (4) Any form of rough play ; (5) Being " off-side " ; (6) Using the wrong hand for throwing.

Penalties.—A penalty for a foul will take the form of a free throw against the offending side from the place where the foul occurred. In the case of rough play, a goal may be allowed against the offending team for each similar offence after the first caution.

Duration of Game.—From 20 to 30 minutes each way, according to the condition of the men.

RECREATIONAL TRAINING

Recreational Training has been compiled mainly for the use of the British Armies in France, but is of general application for other theatres and at home.

(D) RECREATIONAL TRAINING.

The intrinsic value of games lies in their brain-stimulating effect. Troops, after a spell in the trenches, return to the training areas mentally exhausted.

Love of games is inherent in the British race. Games recall the pleasanter circumstances of man's normal existence. The association of ideas they engender creates a happier frame of mind, and the depression born of mental exhaustion and stagnation is counteracted and dispelled.

Men should not be driven to games. An appeal to their sporting instincts will induce them to play, and enthusiasm can be easily aroused by letting them play as the representatives of their units. Games should never be made a parade, as thereby their value is in great part destroyed.

The keenness and the happier atmosphere created by games spread in turn to work, and so a beneficial current is established which reinvigorates the men and allows them to apply to work the concentration necessary to technical training.

When possible, the morning should be devoted to technical training, and the afternoon to games. Thus monotony is avoided, and the men return to work each morning with renewed vitality and increased mental vigour.

PRINCIPLES.

Opportunity for All.

1. One of the first essentials of Recreational Training is that all men should be given the opportunity to take part

in it. In order to do this the following principles must be observed :—

(i) Any form of specialising must be checked which makes players of a few selected experts, while the remainder, who need the training most, look on as mere spectators.

(ii) Platoon teams must be formed for boxing, football, tug-of-war, etc.

(iii) Teams entering cross-country races must consist of unlimited numbers.

(iv) Games must be varied as much as possible, in order that they may appeal to men of every type of physique and temperament.

Competitions should be held in—

Football,	Baseball.
Boxing.	Basketball.
Tug-of-War.	Hockey.
Athletics.	Wrestling, etc.

Championships Arranged.

2. Competitions should be arranged on the championship system, under which men are induced to play and win marks for their units, while the unit which gains the highest number of marks wins the championship. In this way *esprit de corps* is stimulated. Men learn to fight for their unit, and so develop the spirit of self-sacrifice, a spirit which is illustrated by the boxer who gamely faces certain defeat in the ring so that he may win a mark for his unit by " putting up a plucky fight."

2A. Games programmes should be arranged on every course of instruction, even in small Brigade classes. " All-round " championships tend to foster *esprit de corps* and the competitive spirit. A method of marking for " all-round " championships is shown in paras. 122 and 123.

No Money Prizes.

3. Money prizes must not be given. They kill good sport, encourage selfishness and destroy the spirit of individual

sacrifice which games are intended to foster. Trophies, medals and similar souvenirs should be given.

▶ Particulars of prizes which may be obtained in France are given in the Appendix.

ORGANISATION.

Officers Should Take Part.

4. Officers should take a personal and active interest in the games. They will thereby ensure that they are played in the true sporting spirit and at the same time will increase the bond of sympathy between themselves and their men. They will gain too, an insight into the characters of their men which they could obtain by no other means. The success of the Recreational Training Scheme will depend to a very large extent upon the energy displayed in its adoption by the junior officers and N.C.Os., for it is they who are in closest contact with the men, and it is to them the men look for direct leadership.

5. By the fact of taking part in games and competitions officers develop those powers of leadership which are absolutely essential to military success.

Delay Avoided.

6. Recreational Training should begin without delay. Immediately a Division comes out of the line, a programme of training should be so arranged that the afternoons are left free for the men to practise and play off their games and competitions.

7. Owing to the uncertainty of the conditions in which the games may have to be carried out, every advantage must be taken of fine days. During unsuitable weather, arrangements should be made to carry out individual practice and competitions in barns, etc.

8. A Brigade or Battalion can carry out recreational training on similar lines to the Division, companies or platoons forming the units for the Brigade or Battalion competitions respectively.

STAGES OF TRAINING.

Progression.

9. In order to maintain interest in the games and induce all men to take part in them, training should be carried out in progressive stages :—

(i) First Stage.—Platoon games, carried out under Battalion arrangements.

(ii) Second Stage.—Company or battery games, carried out under Brigade arrangements.

(iii) A third stage may follow, in which the winners of Battalion or Brigade events may compete for the Divisional Championship, under Divisional arrangements. The most vital stage however, is the first, in which large numbers, and especially the inexpert, should be induced to participate and the " Platoon spirit " thereby be developed.

Phases of Training.

10. Specimen Programme of Training.

1st day ⎫
2nd ,, ⎪
3rd ,, ⎪
4th ,, ⎬ First Phase, under unit arrangements : Platoon, Battery, etc., games, boxing and wrestling competitions and cross-country runs.
5th ,, ⎪
6th ,, ⎪
7th ,, ⎪
8th ,, ⎪
9th ,, ⎭

10th ,, ⎫ Second Phase, under Brigade arrangements : Preliminary and concluding series of matches and competitions in all purely Brigade championships. If Divisional championships are held, the first round in football competition should be played off on or before the 12th day. If more than 16 units compete it should be played off still earlier. The preliminary series of Divisional Boxing Championships should be fought off on the 13th and 15th days,
11th ,, ⎪
12th ,, ⎬
13th ,, ⎪
14th ,, ⎪
15th ,, ⎭

16th day	Final Phase, under Divisional arrangements : To decide Divisional championships ; semi-final rounds, football.
17th „ 18th „	Assault Training Competitions.
19th „	Final round, football; semi-final and final rounds, boxing.
20th „	Cross-country race.
21st „	Presentation day.

ALLOTMENT OF GROUND.

Personnel.

11. An Area Commandant should be appointed from the Division to allot the playing grounds and assault courses. Where possible, he should be in close proximity to bath and drying rooms. He will take over and issue gear, etc.

12. The Physical and Bayonet Training Instructor attached to each Infantry Brigade will assist in laying out grounds and assault courses, and in the organization and management of games and competitions.

13. An Area Staff should be appointed to act as grounds-men and storekeepers of playing gear. Units should send advance parties to take over grounds and gear.

14. A keen officer should be appointed in each unit to " run " the recreational training and to take charge of all equipment provided for the purpose.

Assistance.

15. Application should be made to the Superintendent of P. and B.T., at H.Q. the Army, for assistance in organising games and competitions, appointment of boxing referees, etc.

16. Transport for teams should be arranged by the Division.

SUPPLY OF MATERIAL.

Bayonet Sacks.

17. Sacks for assault course will be obtained from the Ordnance on a scale of 200 per battalion. Necessary straw

to fill them will be supplied by A.S.C. (20 lbs. per sack).—
G.H.Q. letter O.B. 1211, dated 16.6.16.

Discs.

18. Discs for competitions can be obtained from Army
Printing and Stationery Depots.

Parry Sticks.

19. Parry sticks can be obtained from Superintendent of
P. and B.T., Armies.

Ropes.

20. Tug-of-war ropes can be demanded on loan from
Ordnance —G.H.Q. letter O.S.A. 2/733, dated 5.8 17.

Athletic Kit.

21. Grants of footballs, running shorts and boxing gloves
will be made to :—

 (i) Divisions, Army and Corps Schools, Corps units
 and Reinforcement Camps, on application to
 Superintendents P. and B.T., at Headquarters
 of the Army.
 (ii) Convalescent Depots, on application to Superintendent P. and B.T., Convalescent Depots, at
 H.Q.. P. and B.T.

22. In order to avoid disappointment, units should give
at least 14 days' notice of their requirements in :

 (i) Recreational Training kit and registered cups and
 medals, to Supts. of Armies.
 (ii) Unregistered cups, medals and other prizes, kit on
 repayment, etc., to Officer i/c E.F.C. (Northern),
 G.H.Q., 2nd Echelon. Telegrams :—" Canteens,
 Paris Plage."

ENGRAVING.

22A. Cups and medals will be engraved, free of charge, by
arrangement with Supts. and Asst. Supts. P. and B.T.
Engraving orders are executed in strict rotation.

COMPETITIONS.

ASSAULT TRAINING.

INDIVIDUAL COMPETITION.—(To be carried out under unit arrangements.)

Pointing Practice.

23. Standing, either foot forward, and pointing through ring fixed on end of stick.

> (i) The ring should be held for :—
>
> > (a) One long point, straight forward, out of distance.
> > (b) One short oblique point.
> > (c) One jab.
>
> (ii) Every point must be made with vigour and followed by a vigorous withdrawal. The rifle must be correctly held ("Bayonet Training," Plates II, IV and V).
>
> (iii) Two marks are allowed for each point through the ring. One or both marks are deducted if the point of bayonet hits the side of the ring for a point made without vigour, rifle held incorrectly, or bad withdrawal.

Direction Practice.

24. Charge in open over sacks, trenches, etc. Course not less than 80 yards, for which a standard time should be fixed. Competitors charge magazines with four rounds of blank ammunition. Target discs should be of not less than $1\frac{1}{2}$ in. diameter. Tin rings should have an inside diameter of not less than 4 in.

Start from prone position and fire one round at disc fixed about 1 ft. from tip of bayonet. Run about 40 yards, pointing at three or more rings fixed at varying heights, jumping over obstacles *en route*. Fire one round in standing position at disc. Run a further 40 yards and point at more rings. Finish with two rounds in kneeling position.

    (i) The rifle must be carried in correct " on guard " position.

    (ii) Point must be properly delivered at each ring.

    (iii) Two marks for each hit on the disc and two for each ring bayoneted.

    (iv) Deduct one mark for every second over standard time. To fix standard time take the time of an average man carrying out the practice.

    (v) Deduct marks for points badly made, and for carrying the rifle incorrectly while charging.

Assault Practice—Over Assault Course.

25. Shooting and bayoneting discs fixed on dummies in the open and in trenches.

General Idea.

26. (i)—To open fire at a retreating enemy.

(ii) To advance and assault a number of enemy's lines.

(iii) To occupy a position and open fire against a counter-attack.

Conditions.

27.—(i) Starting position.—Any suitable position. Open fire with blank ammunition (three rounds) at three different discs placed about 5 ft. in front of position. (Discs held in wire bracket attached to small wooden stakes.)

(ii) Enemy's lines.—Represented by a number of dummies on ground, on gallows and in trenches.

(iii) Fire position. A trench or line of shell holes.

(iv) Counter attack. Represented by targets on Stop Butt.

Marking.

28.—(i) Two marks awarded for each disc hit from original fire position.

(ii) Two marks awarded for each disc bayoneted. A competitor who touches a disc with his hand or picks one off the ground with the point of his bayonet will be disqualified.

(iii) Two marks awarded for each hit on the target.

(iv) One mark deducted for each second over standard time fixed.

ROUGH GUIDE TO COURSE.

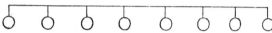

Starting Position

Gallows

Dummies in open
or Shell Holes

Wire

Rough Trench

Targets

Stop Butt

Ties.

29. In the event of a tie the competitor who obtains the highest marks in the assault practice will be given the award. If still equal, the competitor obtaining the highest number of bayonet marks.

TEAM COMPETITION.

30. Dress.—Fighting kit. Team : One officer, four N.C.Os. and 40 privates. Numbers to be arranged by the Division, and to depend on conditions, course, butt, etc.

General Idea.

31.—(i) To advance from a starting point in a series of waves and assault a number of enemy lines.

(ii) To occupy a position and open fire against a counter-attack.

Conditions.

32.—(i) Starting position.—Any suitable position

(ii) Enemy's lines.—Represented by a number of dummies on ground, gallows, in trenches or in shell holes.

(iii) Fire position. In the open or any natural or artificial position.

(iv) Targets on stop butt or miniature range, 30 yards if possible.

(v) Discs should be securely fixed on dummies, between two long stitches of string or wire, to represent vulnerable parts and " openings."

Marking.

33. Target marks awarded :—

    (i) For every hit with blank, 2 marks.

    (ii) For every disc bayoneted, 2 marks.

    (iii) For every hit with bullet, 2 marks.

Control marks allowed :—

    (i) Starting position : 1 mark per man.

    (ii) Enemy's lines : Each position 1 mark per man.

    (iii) Fire position : 1 mark per man.

Ties.

34. In the event of a tie, the team which pierced most discs to be given the award ; if still equal, the team which made most bullet hits.

Points to be observed.

35. Points to be observed :—

   (i) Starting Position.
    (a) Fire control and fire orders.
    (b) Invisibility before advance.
    (c) Quickness in getting away.
    (d) Control in forming line for assault.
    (e) Absence of noise, talking and confusion.

   (ii) Charging enemy in open (dummies on gallows and ground and in shell holes).
    (a) Control of line during advance.
    (b) Dash at moment of contact.
    (c) Vigour of point and withdrawal.
    (d) Control of line after contact.
    (e) Absence of noise and confusion.

   (iii) Charging enemy in trench, through or over obstacles.
    (a) Control of line during advance.
    (b) Dash of line when approaching trench.
    (c) Point of bayonet kept on dummy when in the act of jumping.
    (d) Vigour of withdrawal.
    (e) Control of line after leaving trench.
    (f) Absence of noise and confusion.

   (iv) Fire position.
    (a) Rapidity of taking up position and consolidating.
    (b) Fire orders and control.
    (c) Absence of noise and confusion.

Officials.

36.—(i) There should be a referee, a starter, a timekeeper and a scorer.

(ii) One judge at starting trench, at each line of dummies and at fire position. Judges should deduct marks from maximum allowed for control, and count hits on targets. The same judges should act throughout for same positions.

(iii) There should be a sufficient number of orderlies to fix discs, set up dummies, etc., after each wave goes over the course.

Hints to Judges.

37.—(i) Stand in a position so that the whole line can be seen advancing and at the moment of impact.

(ii) It is easier to count and deduct a mark from each individual who loses control, makes a bad point or withdrawal, talks or shouts, than to attempt to give marks for the men who make correct points.

BOXING.

38. Boxing, which can be carried on either in or out of doors, should begin during the first phase of the training with platoon, company and regimental competitions or inter-regimental matches, in which the representatives for the Divisional Championships may be discovered. In these earlier competitions bouts may be reduced to three rounds of $1\frac{1}{2}$ minutes or 1 minute each, or even to one round of 2 minutes.

39. The following G.R.O. was published on January 7th, 1917 :—

2059.—Boxing.

   (i) All boxing competitions and contests must be carried out under the R.N. and A.B.A. Rules, copies of which can be obtained from H.Q., E.F.C. (Northern) G.H.Q., 2nd Echelon, price 9*d*.

  (ii) *No money prizes may be given.*

 (iii) To cover the expense of the meeting, *e.g.*, hiring of hall, lighting, etc., a small fee may be charged, but this fee should be fixed to such an amount that the total received should not exceed, if possible, the estimated cost of above. On all such occasions a balance-sheet will be kept and forwarded to the Deputy Inspector of Physical and Bayonet Training, at H.Q., P. and B.T., with the profits, should there be any.

39A. The R.N. and A.B.A. rules should be explained by referee to competitors and spectators whom he suspects to be unfamiliar with them.

40. The following are the weights for championships :—

Heavy weight ...	...	catch-weight
Lt.-Heavy weight	...	12st. 7lbs. (175lbs.) and under
Middle weight ...	...	11st. 6lbs. (160lbs.) and under
Welter weight ...	...	10st. 7lbs. (147lbs.) and under
Light weight ...	...	9st. 9lbs. (135lbs.) and under
Feather weight ...	...	9st. 0lbs. (126lbs.) and under
Bantam weight ...	...	8st. 6lbs. (118 lbs.) and under

41. Equivalent French weights :—

Heavy weight ...	...	...	catch-weight
Lt.-Heavy weight	...	...	80 kilos.
Middle weight ...	...	...	73 ,,
Welter weight ...	...	...	67 ,,
Light weight ...	...	...	61 ,,
Feather weight ...	...	...	57 ,,
Bantam weight ...	...	...	53 ,,

41A. If competitors are weighed in uniform (walking-out dress) an addition of 13 lbs. (or 6 kilos.) must be made for clothes.

42. Each unit to be limited to one entry per weight.

43. 8-oz. gloves to be used.

44. Bouts to consist of three 2 minute rounds. When large entries are received, the preliminary series may consist of bouts either of three rounds of 1 minute or one round of 2 minutes.

45. All byes must be in the first series of each weight, and the " draw " so arranged that the number of men left in after the first series will be a power of 2, i.e., 8, 16, 32, etc.

46. A competitor who wins a bout will be awarded two marks towards the aggregate of his unit. A loser who has boxed the full three rounds, has been knocked out, or has been withdrawn by the referee, will be awarded one mark. A competitor drawing a bye or "walking over" will be awarded two marks; if, however, he does not turn out for the next series he shall forfeit the marks awarded for the bye. An extra half-mark may be given to an especially plucky loser.

47. The unit which compiles the highest aggregate marks will gain the championship trophy. In the event of ties, the unit which has most boxers competing to be given the award; if still equal, the award to go to the unit which did best at the lightest weight.

48. A competitor who is disqualified shall forfeit any marks he may have gained prior to his disqualification.

49. A medal should be given to each winner and " runner-up."

49A. Novices' competitions should be fostered in platoons and companies, but every care should be taken to exclude experts from such competitions.

FOOTBALL.

50. Owing to the difficulty of finding suitable grounds it is not always possible to adhere to the dimensions laid down in Army F.A. Rules. Where it is not possible the proportions should be preserved.

51. In all other respects competitions will be played under Army F.A. Rules.

52. Competitions will be decided on the "knock-out" system.

53. Time, 30 minutes each way. In case of a draw, extra time will be played, 10 minutes each way. A second period of extra time will be played, if necessary. If, after the second "extra time," the game is still undecided, it will be played **off next day**

54. All byes must be in the first round, and the "draw" so arranged that the number of teams left in after the first round will be a power of 2, *i.e.*, 8, 16, 32, etc.

55. Referee and linesmen to be neutral.

56. The final round to be played on neutral ground.

56A. Army F.A. Rules may be obtained from Officer i/c E.F.C. (Northern), G.H.Q., 2nd Echelon, price 65c.

ATHLETICS.

57. In athletic meetings only the following standard events should count for marks :—

> 1.—100 yards race.
> 2.—220 yards race.
> 3.—440 yards race.
> 4.—880 yards race.
> 5.—Mile race.
> 6.—120 yards hurdle race.
> 7.—Relay race.
> 8.—Putting the shot.
> 9.—Long jump.
> 10.—High jump.

58. Where it is not possible to obtain a ground, the dimensions of which allow races at the above distances, the following might be substituted as standard events :—

> 1.—Short sprint race instead of 100 yards.
> 2.—Medium sprint race instead of 220 yards.
> 3.—Long sprint instead of 440 yards.
> 4.—3 or 4 Laps instead of 880 yards.
> 5.—6 or 8 Laps instead of 1 mile.

59. Marking for individual events is as follows :—

> 1st   4 marks
> 2nd   3   „
> 3rd   2   „

For relay races :—

> 1st   4 marks per man per team.
> 2nd   3   „   „   „
> 3rd   2   „   „   „

60. Two parallel lines 120 yards long and 63 yards apart, joined at each end by semi-circles, or two parallel lines 100 yards long and 75 yards 21 inches apart, joined at each end by semi-circles, give a track of approximately 440 yards, measured 12 inches inside the flags.

61. It is unwise to attempt to run lap races on tracks of any size other than 220 or 440 yards, as intermediate dimensions involve numerous starting and finishing points. Where a lap of 220 or 440 yards is impossible, it is better to adopt the alternatives indicated above.

62. Tracks shall be marked 10 yards behind the start for 440 yards and 880 yards and mile, and similarly behind the start for 220 yards. In the intervening space, between the start and 10 yards mark, relay runners may take over the flag. If they take over outside that space they are disqualified.

63. The unit which compiles the highest aggregate marks will gain the championship trophy. In the event of ties, the unit which had the most competitors " placed " will be given the award ; if still equal, the award goes to the unit which did best in the track events.

63A. A.A.A. Rules may be obtained from Hon. Sec., A.A.A. 36, King Street, Cheapside, E.C. Price 6d.

CROSS-COUNTRY RUNNING.

64. For cross-country running every effort must be made to avoid cultivated land. Where any doubt or difficulty exists, races over roads and field paths must be substituted. Course about 3½ miles ; never more than 4.

65. Time about 30 minutes for 3½ miles, proportionately less for shorter distances. In order to encourage the slower men, two time limits may be set, one of 30 min. and another of 32 min.

66. Each unit to be allowed to start an unlimited number of competitors.

07. One mark awarded to every runner who finishes within the time limit. If two time limits are set, 2 marks

should be awarded to every runner who finishes within 30 min. and 1 mark to every runner who finishes within 32 min.

68. Thirty minutes or proportionate interval between the starting of each team.

69. The unit which has the highest number of men to complete the course within the time limit to be awarded the championship trophy. In the event of ties, the unit with the highest number of officers completing the course within the time limit to be declared the winner.

70. All competitors will run in boots.

70A. Attempts to find individual winners should be discouraged.

WRESTLING.

71. Wrestling competitions will be held at the following weights :—

Heavy weight	catch-weight
Lt.-Heavy weight ...	12st. 7lbs. (175lbs.) and under
Middle weight	11st. 6lbs. (160lbs.) and under
Welter weight	10st. 7lbs. (147lbs.) and under
Light weight	9st. 9lbs. (135lbs.) and under
Feather weight	9st. 0lbs. (126lbs.) and under
Bantam weight	8st. 6lbs. (118lbs.) and under.

72. Equivalent weights French :—

Heavy weight	catch-weight
Lt.-Heavy weight	80 kilos.
Middle weight	73 ,,
Welter weight	67 ,,
Light weight	61 ,,
Feather weight	57 ,,
Bantam weight	53 ,,

73. The wrestlers may take hold anywhere above the belt, subject to the following restrictions :—The hair, flesh, ears, and clothing may not be seized. Butting with the head or shoulder, and twisting of fingers or thumbs, are forbidden, nor shall any hold be allowed which threatens the breakage or dislocation of a limb, and which may induce the wrestler so held to concede the fall. Kicking is forbidden, but striking with the side of the foot shall not be termed kicking.

74. The " fall " shall be allotted to a wrestler when his opponent touches the ground with any part of his body other than his feet. Although the latter may still retain his hold, he shall not be allowed to continue, but shall be adjudged the loser.

75. If both wrestlers fall to the ground, the man who is first down, or who is undermost, shall be the loser. If they fall simultaneously side by side, or in any fashion that prevents the judges from deciding which was first down, the fall shall be called a " dog fall," and shall have no value for either man.

76. The wrestlers shall compete in stockinged feet or shall wear rubber-soled gymnasium shoes.

77. At every contest or competition there shall be not fewer than two judges who shall arbitrate with the referee. The decision of one judge shall not be accepted, and the referee, when the judges are not unanimous, shall decide. The referee shall have power also to decide any point not provided for by these rules.

78. The referee shall disqualify immediately any man using unfair or illegal methods.

79. If the fall is not obtained within two minutes, the referee, after consulting the judges, shall declare in favour of the contestant who is considered to have attacked most consistently ; but, if it be impossible to differentiate between the pair, the bout shall be declared drawn, and shall be wrestled again.

80. A competitor who wins a match shall be awarded 2 marks, which shall go towards the aggregate of his unit. A loser who completes the contest shall be awarded 1 mark.

A competitor drawing a bye or "walking over" will be awarded two marks ; if, however, he does not turn out for the next series he shall forfeit the marks awarded for the bye.

81. No mark shall be awarded to a competitor who, "scratches" or who retires voluntarily before a decision is reached. His opponent, however, shall still be awarded 2 marks.

82. A competitor who is disqualified shall forfeit any marks he may have gained prior to his disqualification.

TUG OF WAR.

83. Tug of War tournaments should be kept separate from athletic meetings where possible.

84. They should consist of competitions for teams of 10 of the following weights per man :—

Heavy weight	...	...	catch weights.
Middle weight	...	...	11st. (154lbs.) and under.
Light weight	...	...	10st. (140lbs.) „
Feather weight	...	...	9st. (126lbs.) „

85. Equivalent French weights :—

Heavy weight	...	...	...catch weights.
Middle weight	...	...	... 70 kilos.
Light weight	...	...	... 64 „
Feather weight	...	...	... 57 „

86. Each unit will be limited to 1 entry per weight.

87. The rope shall be of sufficient length to allow for a "pull" of 12 feet, with 12 feet of slack at either end, together with 4 feet for each competitor. It should be about 6 inches in circumference. It shall be marked with a single tape tied in the centre.

88. The ground shall be marked with two white lines 24 feet apart, with a centre line marked between them.

89. The rope shall be laid evenly between these lines, and the teams will be lined up on it not closer than 6 feet from the centre mark. The tape on rope shall be directly over

centre mark, or a wooden or wire spring paper clip may be snapped on to rope directly over the centre mark when order to "heave" is given.

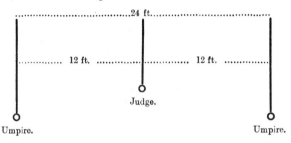

90. The pull shall be 12 feet on either side of the centre line. The winners shall be decided by the best two pulls of three.

91. The team will be considered beaten when the mark on the rope crosses the line of the opposing team.

92. No knots or loops may be made in the rope. The crossing of the rope over itself constitutes a "loop."

93. Boots must be as issued for service, and must not be "faked" in any way.

94. Holes must not be dug in the ground with the feet or otherwise until the word "heave" is given.

95. In all competitions there shall be one judge and two empires. The judge shall start the competition and take charge of the centre and side lines. The umpires shall take charge of the seams and see that the above rules are not infringed.

96. Marking.

1st	...	...	...	...	1 mark per man.	
2nd	...	...	...	...	$\frac{3}{4}$,,	,,
3rd	...	...	...	...	$\frac{1}{2}$,,	,,

MINOR GAMES.

BASKET BALL.

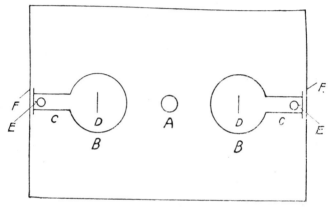

Field of Play.

97. The "field" may be any size up to 4,000 square feet. The width should be two-thirds of the length. A suitable "field" for in or out of doors is 60 feet by 40 feet

A. Centre circle 4 feet in diameter.
B. Two "Lane" circles 12 feet in diameter, with their centre 15 feet from the basket wall at each end of the "field."
C. The "Lane," 6 feet wide, connecting circles with basket wall.
D. The free-throw lines 15 feet from basket wall.
E. The baskets, twice diameter of ball, and 10 feet from ground. There should be a clearance of 6 inches between the basket and the back wall.
F. Backboards, 4 feet high, 6 feet wide. Extend 3 feet above basket.

98. The game is played by 2 teams of 5 players, with an ordinary Association football. Each team endeavours to shoot the ball into its opponent's basket.

99. The members of the team are right and left forwards, centre, and right and left guards. They may move anywhere in the field, and pass the ball in any direction. There is no "off-side."

100. To start the game the referee tosses the ball in the air in the centre circle, but not before the two centres have taken their correct position, *i e.*, heels together and touching the centre circle, with one arm behind the back.

101. The ball tossed by the referee is not in play until it has reached its highest point.

102. A player may dribble the ball with one hand until such time as he takes the ball with both hands, but not after.

103. No player may "travel" whilst holding the ball. "Travelling" consists of making one complete step of any length and in any direction with each foot. If a player in the act of running receives the ball when he has one foot off the ground, he does not complete a step by placing that foot on the ground.

104. A ball out of bounds is returned to play by any opponent of the player who last touched it. The returner may not make a "basket" or again touch the ball until it has been touched by another player. If he holds the ball for more than 4 seconds before returning it to play the ball shall go to the opposite side. When the ball is out of play no player of either team may stand nearer than 3 feet from the line while the throw-in is being taken.

105. Two points shall be given for a "basket" from a "field throw," *i.e.*, any throw when the ball is in play. One point for each "basket" from a "free-throw."

106. A free-throw shall be awarded for each foul by the opposite side. When a free-throw is being taken all but the thrower shall remain outside the "lane" and lane circle. If a player making a free-throw steps over the free-throw line before the "basket" is made no point shall be scored

107. Fouls :—

   (*a*) Holding, tackling, tripping or barging an opponent.

   (*b*) Kicking the ball.

   (*c*) Travelling.

   (*d*) Punching the ball with the fist.

   (*e*) A third man entering a " dispute." The foul is committed immediately he touches the ball.

   (*f*) Dribbling, except with one hand.

   (*g*) Unnecessary roughness.

   (*h*) A player stepping inside the lane or lane circle before the ball has made or missed the basket from a free throw.

   (*j*) Persistently or intentionally delaying the game.

IMPROVISED BASE BALL.

108. Played with an improvised ball, 9 players a side, viz. : Pitcher, catcher, short stop, 1st base, 2nd base, 3rd base, Right field, centre field, left field.

FIELD.

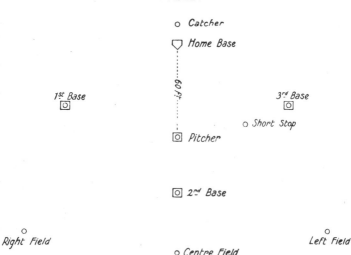

109. The object of the game is to score runs. A run is scored only when the runner completes the circuit of the four bases.

110. The ball is put into play by the "pitcher." It may be pitched with either hand. The "pitcher's box," or place from which he throws the ball shall be 60 feet from the home base if a hard ball is used ; a proportionately shorter distance with a soft ball.

111. If the ball crosses over the home base, between the knees and shoulders of the batter, it shall be called a "strike," even though the batter does not attempt to strike. Three strikes put the man out. Three men out put the whole side out.

112. If the pitcher throws four balls that do not cross the "home base" between the knees and shoulders of the batter, the batter is entitled to take one base.

113. The ball must be batted between 1st and 3rd bases, otherwise it is a "foul" and the batter may not run.

114. Fouls count as "strikes" for the first two strikes. The third or last strike must be a clean miss or be called a "strike" by the umpire.

115. The umpire calls each ball thrown either a "strike" or a "ball."

116. When the ball is hit into the air and is caught by a member of the opposing team the batter is out, and all the men on bases must remain at, or return to, the bases they occupied when the ball was hit.

117. The men on bases cannot advance on a foul ball, but must remain at their bases, until the ball has been returned to the pitcher.

118. The runner is out if he is touched by the ball held by any member of the opposing team, or if the ball is thrown to the member of the opposing team on the base to which he is running. The latter must catch the ball before the runner gets to the base. If he drops it the runner is safe.

119. NOTE.—Players in the field should use their wits, and should do all they can to prevent the opposing side

from scoring. They should throw in the ball to the base at which it will do most good, not necessarily the nearest. The players of the batting team should help their team-mates to get from base to base. In this, as in all other games, the player must play for his side and not for individual distinction.

HOCKEY WITH TENNIS BALL.

120. Hockey can be played upon a very small pitch when a tennis ball is substituted for the ordinary ball. The team can be reduced to five and six a side, and the time cut down to ten minutes each way.

Correct hockey-sticks are not necessary. Any short crook-handled stick cut from a hedge will serve. Hits with either side of the stick should be allowed, otherwise the ordinary rules will govern the games.

FOOTBALL WITH TENNIS BALL.

121. This, too, can be played upon a small pitch, with the goal and areas proportionately reduced. Teams and time may be cut down as for hockey, and the rules governing five and six a side tournaments applied.

ALL-ROUND CHAMPIONSHIP.

METHOD OF MARKING.

1.—For Separate Competitions.

122. Marks should be awarded according to paras. mentioned, and as below :—

MAJOR EVENTS.

Competition.

Team Assault Training	... Paras. 33 and 34.
Boxing	,, 46, 47 and 48.
Wrestling	,, 80, 81 and 82
Football ⎫ Winning team in each match, 2 marks	
Tug-of-War ⎬ for its unit.	
Hockey ⎭ Losing team, 1 mark.	
Cross country	Para. 67

MINOR EVENTS.

Individual Assault Training   ...   Paras. 23, 24 and 28.
Medicine Bag Badminton   ⎫
Rope Quoit Badminton   ⎪   Winning team in each
Bomb Ball   ⎬   match, 2 marks for its
Basket Ball   ⎪   unit.
Base Ball   ⎭   Losing team, 1 mark.

2.—For All-Round Championship.

123. Championship marks are allotted in " Major Events "
at the rate of 2, and in " Minor Events " at the rate of 1 for
each competing team or unit.

Example : 4 units competing.

(*a*) Major Events.—Winning team or unit 8 ; second 6 ;
third 4 ; and fourth 2 marks.

(*b*) Minor Events.—Winning team or unit 4 ; second 3 ;
third 2 ; and fourth 1 mark.

ALL-ROUND CHAMPIONSHIP TABLE FOR A COMPANY.

Platoon.	MAJOR EVENTS.							MINOR EVENTS.						Total Marks.	Placing.
	Team Assault Training.	Boxing.	Cross-Country Race.	Wrestling.	Football.	Tug-of-War.	Hockey.	Individual Assault Trng.	Basket Ball.	Rope Quoit Badminton.	Bomb Ball.	Medicine Bag Badminton.	Base Ball.		
1	6	6	6	4	6	6	6	3	2	2	3	3	2	55	1st
2	8	4	4	8	8	4	4	2	3	1	2	1	3	52	2nd
3	2	8	8	2	2	2	8	1	1	3	1	2	1	41	4th
4	4	2	2	6	4	8	2	4	4	4	4	4	4	52	3rd

No. 1 Platoon did not win a single competition, but showed best all-round efficiency and so won championship.

Nos. 2 and 4 tied but the former gained more marks in Major Events and so took priority.

APPENDIX.

PRIZES.

The registered cups and medals shown below may be obtained, under the authority of Supts. P. and B.T., at H.Q. of the Army, from the Officer i/c E.F.C. (Northern), G.H.Q., 2nd Echelon (Telegrams : "Canteens, Paris Plage "), or, in emergency, directly from H.Q., P. and B.T.

All prices shown are current only at time of issue of this pamphlet, and are subject to the fluctuations of the market.

In order to avoid disappointment, units should give at least 14 days' notice of their requirements in unregistered cups, medals and other prizes, kit, etc., on repayment, to Officer i/c E.F.C. (Northern), G.H.Q., 2nd Echelon (Telegrams : " Canteens, Paris Plage "), and in registered cups and medals to Supts. P. and B.T., at H.Q. of the Army.

Although the intrinsic value of the registered cups and medals is not great, it should be noted that :—

   (i) *The dies from which these are cast will be destroyed after the war, and reproductions will then be unobtainable.*
   (ii) *That names of winners of these trophies are entered at H.Q., P. and B.T., and a permanent record of their performances is kept.*

ENGRAVING.

Cups and medals of all kinds will be engraved, free of charge, by arrangement with Supts. and Asst. Supts. P. and B.T.

Engraving orders are executed in strict rotation, and some little time must elapse between receipt and completion of order.

RECORDS OF WINNERS.

Names of winners (both of individuals and of units) of all registered cups and medals must be forwarded to H.Q., P. and B.T., for registration in " Records of Winners." This applies to all prizes mentioned in paras. I to V,

I—REGISTERED RECREATIONAL TRAINING CUPS

No. 1.

No. 2.

No. 3.

No. 1 Silver ... ... 170fr. 50c.
     Silver Plated ... 68fr. 50c.
     Bronze... ... 68fr. 50c.

No. 2 Silver ... ... 205fr. 00c.
     Silver Plated ... 76fr. 00c.
     Bronze... ... 76fr. 00c.

No. 3 Silver ... ... 211fr. 50c.
     Silver Plated ... 71fr. 50c.
     Bronze... ... 71fr. 50c.

Conditions Governing Presentation of R.T. Cups.

1st Class (Silver)—May be given for :—
1. Divisional Inter-unit championships.
2. Army Schools championships

2nd Class (Silver Plated)—May be given for :—
1. Brigade Inter-unit championships.
2. Corps Schools championships.

3. Six rounds Boxing Contests, in which one of the contestants has won a 1st or 2nd class R.N. and A.B.A. medal.

3rd Class (Bronze)—May be given for :—
1. Regimental team championships and inter-regimental athletic, boxing, cross country, etc., matches.
2. Four rounds and three rounds contests, in which one of the contestants holds a R.N. and A.B.A. medal.

II.—REGISTERED RECREATIONAL TRAINING BUGLES.

Silver Plated Bugles in case, 100fr. 50c.

Conditions Governing Presentation for R.T. Bugles.

R.T. Bugles may be given for :—
1. Divisional Inter-unit championships.
2. Brigade Inter-unit championships.
3. Army Schools championships.
4. Corps Schools championships.

III.—REGISTERED RECREATIONAL TRAINING MEDALS.

Obverse.	Reverse.
1⅝-in. Silver, 14fr. 00c.	1⅝-in. Bronze, 6fr. 00c.
1¼-in. Silver, 9fr. 50c.	1¼-in. Bronze, 3fr. 50c.

Conditions Governing Presentation of R.T. Medals.

1st Class (1⅝-in. Silver and Bronze)—**May be given for :—**

1. All competitions open to units larger than a Brigade.
2. Regimental championships.
3. Army Schools championships.

2nd Class (1¼-in. Silver and Bronze)—May be given for :—

1. All competitions open to regiments or their equivalents.
2. Competitions at Corps Schools, Depot Bns., or their equivalents.
3. Company championships.

N.B.—1st and 2nd class may be given for boxing competitions open to units smaller than a brigade.

IV.—REGISTERED R.N. AND A.B.A. MEDALS.

Obverse.	Reverse.
1¾-in. Silver, 21fr. 50c.	1¾-in. Bronze, 7fr. 50c.
1¼-in. Silver, 9fr. 50c.	1¼-in. Bronze, 4fr. 50c.

Conditions Governing Presentation of Reg. R.N. and A.B.A. Medals.

1st Class (1¾-in. Silver and Bronze)—May be given for :—

Boxing Competitions open to Divisions or larger formations.

2nd Class (1¼-in. Silver and Bronze)—May be given for :—

1. Boxing competitions open to Brigades.
2. Army Schools.

V.—REGISTERED ASSAULT TRAINING MEDALS.

Obverse.	Reverse.
2-in. Silver, 22fr. 00c.	2-in. Bronze, 10fr. 00c.

Conditions Governing Presentation of Assault Training Medal.

May be given for :—

1. Competitions open to units larger than a Brigade.
2. Regimental championships.
3. Army Schools championships.

VARIOUS PRIZES.

VI.—Plain Medals.

Obverse.	Reverse.
1⅝-in. Silver, 9fr. 50c.	1⅝-in. Bronze, 3fr. 00c.
1¼-in. Silver, 8fr. 00c.	1¼-in. Bronze, 2fr, 75c.

The above medals may be purchased, without authority, from Officer i/c E.F.C. (Northern), G.H.Q., 2nd Echelon, or may be obtained in emergency from Supts. P. and B.T. of Armies, or at Headquarters, P. and B.T.

They may be given for any event.

VII.—Miscellaneous.

Prizes, which may be obtained from Officer i/c E.F.C. (Northern), G.H.Q., 2nd Echelon, without authority, are :—

Silver and Silver Plated Cups, from 20 to 250 fr.
Watches.
Razors.
Cigarette cases.
Tobacco boxes.
Pocket knives, etc.

VIII.—A variety of artistic French medals and plaquettes in bronze for running, boxing, swimming, fencing, wrestling and football can also be purchased from Officer i/c E.F.C. (Northern), G.H.Q., 2nd Echelon.

IX.—Recreational Training Kit.

The following articles may be obtained on repayment from Officer i/c E.F.C. (Northern), G.H.Q., 2nd Echelon :—

Boxing Gloves	...	...	18.00 to 25.00 fc. per set.
Cricket Gear ...	...	...	—
Footballs, Association & Rugby			16.00 to 20.00 fc. each.
Football Shirts	...	...	4.50 fc. and upwards.
,, Boots	...	...	—
Hockey Sticks	...	...	—
,, Balls	...	...	—
Spare bladders	...	...	2.75 to 3.50 fc. each.
Shorts	...	...	2.75 to 3.00 fc. per pair.
Gymnasium Shoes	...	...	2.50 to 3.50 fc. per pair.
Gymnasium Vests	...	...	1.50 to 2.00 fc. each.
Jerseys	...	...	2.75 to 3.50 fc. each.
Medicine balls	...	...	22.50 fc. each and upward.
Punchpads	...	...	67.00 fc. each and upward.

8

Hints on Assault, Physical and Recreation Training, 1918

Assault training was a form of recreational training which, like all other games and recreational activities, provided troops with a welcome alternative to their daily duties and life in the trenches. Assault training was also a means of continuing physical training in general, and specifically bayonet training. The pamphlet reproduced in the previous chapter provided instruction on recreational training, which included assault; the following reproduced manual was printed specifically for the Third Army (home of the Physical & Bayonet Training Headquarters) and, as the title suggests, provided hints on conducting assault and recreational training.

THIRD ARMY.

HINTS ON ASSAULT, PHYSICAL AND RECREATIONAL TRAINING.

1914 - 1918 WAR

October, 1918.

PREFACE.

The instructions in this pamphlet are intended principally for the use of P. and B.T. instructors, but they will be found useful by Officers and N.C.O.s who are keen on running recreational and other competitions.

The organization of the competitions is arranged to allow of large numbers competing in a limited time.

PRESS A—9/18—7487E—1,000.

INDEX.

PART I.—ASSAULT TRAINING.

PART II.—PHYSICAL TRAINING.

PART III.—RECREATIONAL TRAINING.

PART IV.—SPECIAL TIPS TO INSTRUCTORS.

PART I.—ASSAULT TRAINING.

1.—COMPETITIONS.

Competitions are a great stimulus to training, yet instructors take A.T. parades day after day and seldom run competitions. Why?

You will get more work, life, energy and interest in A.T., if you will run some form of competition on practically every A.T. parade.

Running competitions is purely a matter of organization. The instructor who tries to do everything himself will achieve nothing. He must detail Officers, N.C.O.s and the men themselves to act as officials.

Four forms of competitions are dealt with here, but others will suggest themselves. Do remember that any form of competition is good, and that there is no idea of tying you down absolutely to the four competitions below:

     (1) Simple bullet and bayonet ;
     (2) Individual A.T. competition ;
     (3) Team A.T. competition ;
     (4) A.R.A. competition.

2.—SIMPLE BULLET AND BAYONET COMPETITIONS.

Appoint a judge (a Private, a N.C.O. or an Officer) for every group competing. This judge will be responsible also that blank ammunition only is served out for Nos. 1, 2 and 4 competitions.

You must also detail a man to serve out ammunition and to replace targets for every group.

Then, if you personally supervise the show, working with a whistle, you will get through these competitions quite quickly, and with perfect safety.

Results should be publicly announced after every competition ; or, better still, shown on a blackboard or canvas frame.

Give a man or team that has done exceptionally well a good chit.

The rules are as follows :

3.—SIMPLE BULLET AND BAYONET COMPETITION.

The following competitions can be run on the usual Assault and Tin Ring Courses, but may be modified to suit local conditions.

Each competition can be run (1) As individual competitions, four to six men competing at one time ; (2) As intersection competitions, four men of each section forming the team, and two teams competing.

General Object.—To develop speed and accuracy, and to stimulate interest in Assault Training.

Method of Conducting.—Competitors or teams fall in at the " Order " at starting point, facing respective dummies. On the command or signal to fire or advance, they will load, fire or advance, charge dummies, etc.

Scoring for Individual Competitions.—

For speed	...	First man to finish	...	2 marks.
		Second man to finish	...	1 marks.
For accuracy	...	Each hit with blank or bullet	...	2 marks.
		Each disc or tin ring bayoneted ...	...	2 ,,

Scoring for Team Competitions.

| For speed | ... | First team to finish | ... | 1 mark per man. |
| For accuracy | ... | As for individual competition. | | |

No. 1. Start in starting trench, fire two rounds blank at discs on parapet, charge dummies at first gallows, delivering long and short points and jab, finishing two paces beyond gallows.

No. 2. Start ten paces in rear of practice trench, charge dummies in trench (position of dummies to be varied), advance to second gallows and fire two rounds of blank at small discs clipped into sides of dummies.

The firing of second round by individual men or by last man of team will place men or teams.

No. 3. Start ten paces in rear of bank, load with one clip, charge dummies on far side of trench, charge to fire position and fire at brick bats, jam tins or other improvised targets. The knocking over of the targets will place men or teams.

No. 4 (at Tin Ring Course). Lie down at fire position, load with three rounds of blank, fire two rounds at discs, rise, charge and point at one or two tin rings, advance to next fire position and fire remaining round at disc standing. The firing of third round by individual men or by last man of team will place men or teams.

N.B.—The above competitions are quick and snappy; they are stimulating, dealing in turn with all kinds of points, fire positions, trenches and obstacles.

With ordinary precautions the four different competitions can be run simultaneously where the average Assault and Tin Ring Courses are available. By changing sections over the men will deal in turn with various phases of the Assault.

4.—INDIVIDUAL A.T. COMPETITION.

Get all the Officers and N.C.O.s you can to judge every phase of this competition. When you are satisfied that Officers and N.C.O.s know how to judge, get the men to act as judges.

If you haven't got time to run right through every phase in one day, do the pointing at rope ring one day, the butt strokes and disarms the next, and so on.

This part of the competition, run by sections, can replace quickeners. The Officers, N.C.O.s or men will do the actual judging. You yourself will supervise and help.

When the best two men of each section have been found, arrange a grand final competition among them.

The judges should shout out the marks after every point or stroke. Don't allow them to get away in a corner marking up mysteriously in a book : have the thing open and above board. If the men know why they have dropped marks, they will try to correct their faults. The competition then becomes educational.

For the more informal competitions it isn't even necessary to record the marks on paper ; simply ask the men to memorise the marks allotted to them.

At the finish ask who has a possible, one below possible, so on, and fight off the ties where necessary.

For the pointing at rope ring, butt strokes and disarm, the judge calls out : "Two!" "One!" or "Nothing!" for each point, stroke, &c., according to performance. The scorer enters up the score.

An Officer, N.C.O. or man presents the ring, or the blob, or he attacks the competitor for the disarm.

To make the conditions equal and fair for each competitor, the ring ought to be presented in one way for all the competitors; but a different sequence of points can be arranged at each competition.

At the Tin Ring Course you will want a referee, two judges, a starter and timekeeper, a scorer, and men detailed to replace targets and tin rings. (As correct pointing at tin rings is insisted on, these must be fairly large; the hole should be as large as a bayonet disc.)

The starter gives the order or signal for each man to start, and also times the run. He reports to the referee either "Time correct" or so many seconds over.

The referee stands in middle of course and watches the targets hit with blank, the tin rings bayoneted and announces at the end :—

> 6 marks for the rifle.
> 12 marks for the bayonet.
> 1 mark deducted for one second over time.
> 2 marks deducted for bad position of on guard, lack of go in pointing &c.;
> Total 15.

The scorer enters up score on form. It is best to have a judge on either side of course (outside) whom the referee may appeal to in case of doubt as to whether a ring has been bayoneted or not. But, if the referee moves up and down as the competitor runs over the course, he will very seldom have to appeal to the judges.

For the Assault Practice the following Officials are required :—

> A referee.
> A starter.
> A timekeeper.
> Two judges.
> A scorer. Men to replace targets and discs.

The referee takes up a position from which he can see the whole performance. The first judge watches the competitor at starting position, first gallows, and practice trench, and returns to the referee the marks for the rifle and bayonet.

The second judge watches results at second gallows, bank and at fire position, and returns to the referee the marks for the bayonet and the rifle.

The timekeeper tells referee "Time correct," or so many seconds over.

(The standard time for the competitions must be arrived at by actual trials.)

If the referee notes in his book under the two heads as follows :—

	R (rifle)	B (bayonet)
1st Judge	6	8
2nd Judge	10	4

he can then announce 16 for the rifle and 12 for the bayonet.

He should also announce deductions for over time or bad performance, leaving a total for the scorer to enter on form.

Sixteen men have gone through every phase of the individual A.T. Competition in 35 minutes. Try to beat that. Of course, by passing men on from Rope Ring to Tin Ring Course, and on to Assault Course, and all going on at the same time, a great deal of time can be saved.

The score sheet, plan of Tin Ring Course and of Assault course are shown.

5.—RECORD FORM FOR INDIVIDUAL ASSAULT TRAINING COMPETITION.

Platoon or Coy.	Rank.	Name.	Rope Ring	Butt Strokes	Disarm	Direction Practice	Assault Practice	Total.	Placing.	Remarks.
			Long and short points and jab. Two marks for each thrust thro' ring. Deduct one or both for faults.	Two marks. Deduct one or both for faults.	Two marks. Deduct one or both for faults.	(1) Fire one round blank lying. (2) Point at four rings. (3) Fire one round blank Standing. (4) Point at four rings. (5) Fire one round blank kneeling. Two marks for each disc hit and two for each ring bayoneted. Deduct one mark for every second over time and deduct also for faults.	(1) Fire three rounds blank. (2) Charge down Course bayoneting discs. (3) Fire five live rounds at targets. Two marks for each disc hit with blank. Two marks for each disc bayoneted. Two marks for each hit on target. Deduct one mark for every second over time and deduct also for faults.			

The long headings need not be reproduced on forms actually required for competitions. They are put in this pro-forma for information and guidance. Full information regarding this type of competition will be found on pages 9, 10 and 11 RECREATIONAL TRAINING (*Revised Edition*). Butt strokes and one disarm are introduced to make competition more thorough. Parries may be introduced also.

Date.. ....*Referee.*

6.—TIN RING ASSAULT COURSE.

THIS PLAN IS MERELY A GUIDE :- STRAIGHT, ZIG-ZAG OR LETTER S COURSE MAY BE USED INSTEAD

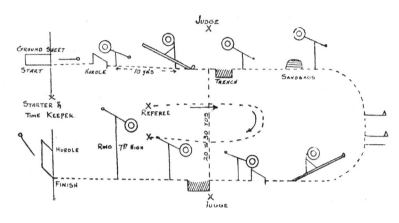

CONDITIONS. Lying at the start, rifle loaded, with three rounds. Blank. At "go" fire one round lying at cardboard disc, rise, and bayonet tin rings down first side of course, stop between flags, fire one round standing at disc, proceed down second side of course, bayonet tin rings at finish, fire over hurdle one remaining round at discs kneeling.

TIME Taken from word "Go" to last round being fired

MARKING Two marks for each disc hit with Blank.
Two marks for each tin ring bayoneted.
One point to be deducted for each second overtime
Blank targets 1¼" diameter. Tin rings must be fairly large.

NOTE :- Correct "On Guard" position must be maintained and points vigorously delivered at rings.

7.—ASSAULT TRAINING COURSE.

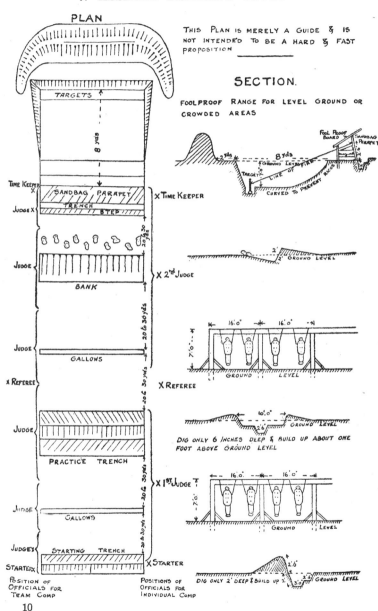

PLAN

THIS PLAN IS MERELY A GUIDE & IS NOT INTENDED TO BE A HARD & FAST PROPOSITION

SECTION.

FOOLPROOF RANGE FOR LEVEL GROUND OR CROWDED AREAS

TARGETS

8 YDS

TIME KEEPER
SANDBAG PARAPET
TRENCH
JUDGE
STEP
X TIME KEEPER

FOOL PROOF BOARD
SANDBAG PARAPET
2 YDS
8 YDS
GROUND LEVEL
LINE OF FIRE
TARGET
CURVED TO PREVENT RICO.

20 & 30 YDS

JUDGE
BANK
X 2ND JUDGE

2'
2' GROUND LEVEL

20 & 30 YDS

JUDGE
GALLOWS

X REFEREE
X REFEREE

16'. 0"   16'. 0"
7'. 0"
GROUND   LEVEL

20 & 30 YDS

JUDGE
PRACTICE TRENCH

16'. 0"
2'.6"   GROUND LEVEL

DIG ONLY 6 INCHES DEEP & BUILD UP ABOUT ONE FOOT ABOVE GROUND LEVEL

20 & 30 YDS

JUDGE
GALLOWS
X 1ST JUDGE

16'. 0"   16'. 0"
7'. 0"
GROUND   LEVEL

20 & 30 YDS

JUDGE
STARTING TRENCH
STARTER
X STARTER

2'.6"
3'.0"   2'.6"   GROUND LEVEL

DIG ONLY 2' DEEP & BUILD UP 2'

POSITION OF OFFICIALS FOR TEAM COMP

POSITIONS OF OFFICIALS FOR INDIVIDUAL COMP

10

8.—TEAM ASSAULT TRAINING COMPETITION.

Get a number of Army Books 153B—one for each judge—with "Starting Trench," "First Gallows," "Fire Position," etc. on outside of cover. On the inside of cover write out the "Points to be observed," and maximum marks allowed for control, discs, etc.

Give the judges their respective books, place them in position showing each his job: i.e., his own area of course, as indicated on plan—where to place himself whilst following each team, etc.

The teams should be formed up behind starting trench, opened out, ammunition served out—ready to take up position in starting trench.

As soon as the first team starts the second team gets into starting trench.

The instant one team is clear of course and targets are replaced, the next team should be started.

Each judge first marks up his fire orders, control and dash marks, then counts hits on targets or discs bayoneted, and, finally, totals marks in readiness to return to scorer.

When all the teams have finished, judges assemble and give the various scores to scorer. Referee decides what marks to allot for time.

Twelve teams have gone through the competition on quite a big course in 34 minutes. Try and beat that by tip-top organization. If you can show senior Officers that this competition can be run without waste of time, they will see that these competitions are frequently held. But with bad organization and consequent waste of time, they are allowed to drop out. It is up to you to show how quickly this competition can be run off.

Always provide sufficient men to replace discs and targets quickly.

The score sheet which follows gives all the particulars necessary:—

9.—RECORD FORM FOR TEAM ASSAULT TRAINING COMPETITION.

	TEAMS.			
STARTING TRENCH.				One mark for each bayonet man allowed for fire orders, control, etc. Two marks for each disc hit with blank.
FIRST GALLOWS.				One mark for each bayonet man allowed for control, etc. Two marks for each disc pierced by a proper point.
CENTRE TRENCH.				Do.
SECOND GALLOWS.				Do.
LAST TRENCH OR BANK.				Do.
FIRE POSITION.				One mark for each bayonet man allowed for fire orders, control, etc. Two marks for every hit on target.
MARKS for TIME.				Time of each team to be taken. Two marks for each bayonet-man allowed for fastest team and a smaller proportion to other teams according to time, at discretion of Referee.
TOTALS				

Judges must deduct freely from maximum marks allowed for control, etc., for each individual fault seen. A disc does not count when a man stops and takes it deliberately.

PLACING 1st ....

        2nd ....

        3rd ....

                              Referee.

                              ....

Officials Required.—A Referee, a Starter, a Timekeeper, a Scorer. One Judge at Starting Trench, one at Fire Position, and one at each line of dummies.

A sufficient number of orderlies to replace discs and targets quickly.

Five minutes' explanation to Officials as to points to look out for (shown below) and there ought to be no trouble in getting the required number of Officers to officiate. In fact, it is their job.

POINTS TO BE OBSERVED AND MARKS DEDUCTED FOR:—

Starting Position.

Faulty fire control, orders and positions.

Men showing over parapet before advance.

Slowness in getting away.

Faulty control of line during advance.

Noise, talking and confusion.

First Gallows.

Faulty control of line during advance.

Want of dash at moment of contact.

Lack of vigour in pointing and withdrawing.

Faulty control of line after contact.

Noise, talking and confusion.

Middle Trench.

Faulty control of line during advance.

Want of dash when approaching trench.

Point of bayonet not kept on dummy when in act of jumping.

Incorrect or slack withdrawal. (Foot should be placed on dummy).

Faulty control of line after leaving trench.

Noise, talking and confusion.

Second Gallows.

As for first Gallows.

Second Trench or Bank.

As for Middle Trench.

Fire Position.

Slowness in taking up position.

Faulty fire control, orders and positions.

Noise, talking and confusion.

Team competitions should be fostered. Get keen Officers to challenge other Platoons or Companies. Don't wait for a stereotyped course ; improvise one anywhere. *Gallows are not essential.*

9a.—INFORMAL TEAM A.T. COMPETITION.

Where it is desired to run an informal competition among a number of waves quite quickly, and there are not enough Officers and N.C.O.s to act as judges, &c., in the usual manner, the senior Officer or instructor present can allot up to a maximum of 100 marks per wave for fire orders, control, dash, &c., over the whole course.

He should deduct freely from that maximum in tens or twenties according to performance. In addition to the 100 marks or proportion thereof, hits on targets and discs bayoneted should be counted in the usual way.

Wave with highest aggregate wins.

10.—A.R.A. COMPETITION.

The conditions of the competition are published in a separate pamphlet.

A.G. Staff Instructors should prepare the course (three irregular rows of dummies) at the laid down distances, arrange for orderlies to replace discs (between twine stitches), and prepare a score sheet, *pro forma* as below:—

11.—SCORE SHEET FOR ARMY RIFLE ASSOCIATION COMPETITION.

Marks Awarded.

	PLATOONS.				
	No. 1	No. 2	No. 3	No. 4	
First Row of dummies					2 marks for each disc bayoneted (D not allow a disc to count where a man stops and takes it deliberately).
Second Row of dummies					
Third Row of dummies					
Hits on targets. ...					1 mark for each hit on target.
Total ...					

Marks Deducted.

	PLATOONS				
	No. 1	No. 2	No. 3	No. 4	
For firing after whistle					2 marks for every round fired after whistle.
For faulty command and control, lack of dash, faulty pointing and withdrawing, noise and confusion.					1 or more marks up to 66. (Deduct freely for all faults seen).
Total ...					

Net Marks.

Marks awarded ...					
Marks deducted ...					
NET TOTAL ...					

Placing.—First..............................

Second............................

Third.............................

Fourth ....

Date...........................   ....Referee.

12.—TIPS FOR ASSAULT COURSES.

The plan of assault course is intended merely to be a guide, and should not be slavishly reproduced. Gallows are not essential.

(1) First of all try to find a natural stop butt, where you can have a 30^X range.

(2) Where the ground is flat or in crowded areas, be satisfied with an 8^X or 10^X range and fire under a fool-proof roof.

(3) Don't dig deep trenches for assault courses. If you dig down 2' you will get enough sods and earth to build up to a height of 4' 6". The sides of trenches should be battered ; they will stand ever so much longer, and need less revetting.

(4) Always build as wide a course as possible—20 or 30 dummies in each row—as little or no leadership is required to control a wave of six or eight men.

(5) Wherever possible have at least 30^x between the various rows of dummies.

(6) Trenches and gallows need not be in beautifully straight lines or absolutely parallel.

(7) Make use of any natural obstacles, such as sunken roads, ditches, banks, etc.

(8) Be ingenious, and reproduce "No Man's Land" by means of shell holes, wire, etc., but don't have these obstacles round the gallows at which you may want to do some elementary work in comfort.

(9) Gallows should never be more than 7' high, or you will find it awkward to refix dummies.

(10) A good method of fixing parry sticks in dummies is to stick them right through the dummies with one single wire fixed to stick close to face of dummy and to cross bar.

3' x 1' 6"

(11) Improvise courses wherever you go. First find a stop butt, then place rows of dummies on ground, suspended to trees, between stakes or nailed on boards in pairs as in sketch, and placed in irregular rows all over the course.

An oil drum filled with sand at bottom of sack makes an excellent upstanding movable dummy.

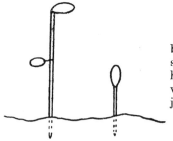

For targets use jam tins, brickbats, bottles, &c. When short of sacks use training sticks of various heights, as shown in sketch, at which long and short points and jab could be made.

(12) On grounds where it is safe to fire from 150^x range don't erect gallows on course, use dummies on ground, etc.; make teams fire live ammunition from jump-off; go over course with magazines loaded, safety catches back, and then open fire again whenever necessary. The gallows for elementary work can be erected on spare ground clear of course. An assault course is generally a clear indication of an Instructor's worth.

(13) Where Assault Courses have to be constructed on flat ground, reduce frontage of fire position to 3' per man, and the stop butt to 2' per target. This will save a large amount of digging.

An Instructor with initiative will have falling dummies, butt stroke dummies, etc., and his course will always be in good order.

13.—GENERAL INSTRUCTIONS.

The men we have to deal with in France are at the very least semi-trained, and must be recognized as such. Too many instructors appear to regard them as raw recruits, and start every lesson with work by word of command. DON'T!

Pointing at thin air day after day kills interest, and takes all fight out of the training.

All lessons should be fighting lessons, BOCHE KILLING practices, and not merely drills.

DON'T TALK, but give the men lots of practice.

Commence always with a counter charge practice. From that get to work with training sticks, men working in pairs, or in small circles of 6 or 8, every man taking a turn at handling the stick. Men who have been taught to train themselves will act for themselves in a fight.

After this get to work on dummies. If there are not enough to go round on gallows, have rows of them on spare ground, and let the men practise pointing at these dummies, at a walk, at a run and charging. Don't forget direction practice. Always give a distinct target to aim at. Use discs frequently. A splendid practice on gallows is that of going along the row of dummies delivering long and short points, butt strokes, jabbing and kicking, and fairly working the men up to go all out. Call this the mad half minute, and carry it out daily.

Plant cleft sticks at an angle in the ground, in irregular rows, place tin rings in the clefts and get the men to charge and bayonet the tin rings; or get men to hold out the sticks whilst others practise charging. Remember, this practice is to foster dash, so make the men go like blazes.

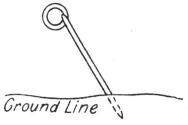

Ground Line

Firing practices must not be neglected. Get the sympathy and assistance of the musketry experts, so as to run these practices on sound lines, and get plenty of actual firing carried out.

Finish all lessons with either the Final Assault or with a counter charge practice. Counter charge every ten minutes at all lessons.

Remember to make a series of lessons progressive, so that after a few days' training only advanced work and competitions are taken. Short, snappy lessons of half-an-hour's duration are the best.

Insist on correct arms drill movements, correct marching off, inspection of arms, marching out of fire positions, etc. If a drill command is given, only correct drill is permissible; but when quick changes of positions are given or in quickening exercises the order should be "move!" When individuals are called out to take a lesson, insist on dash and life. The return to the class should also be smart and soldier-like.

The high port is a method of carrying the rifle preparatory to the assault, and not one to be used when marching from one place to another. In the latter case use the slope. When advancing to the attack over a long distance, trail arms.

When in or near enemy lines remain on guard. Don't return to high port after every point; keep on guard.

Training sticks must be well made with a small blob at one end and a wire ring covered with string at the other. Wire by itself does not make a good target, it is not seen easily enough. The ring should be 4″ in diameter.

Training sticks must be available in large numbers on all A.T. Parades. Staff Instructors are responsible for this. Jab sacks must be fixed to give absolutely horizontal targets on all gallows.

Sand bags or bundles of sticks must be available for consolidating in both fire positions.

Targets are to be painted on both sides of dummies. This can be done most easily before sacks are filled.

These targets are purely for elementary practice. For all Final Assault Practices DISCS must be used.

Double stitches of twine must be sown into all dummies so that discs may be readily and quickly replaced.

Make double wire clips of this size (no larger) for blank targets. Pieces of cardboard of the same size, to fit neatly in, will readily be blown away by a blank round.

If the targets are larger, the aiming and trigger pressing become careless.

These targets should be placed fairly wide apart, and should be of varying heights, to ensure change of aim practice.

Wherever there is a permanent Assault Course instructors must fix up disappearing targets.

When units on the move cannot transport Assault Training gear, Staff Instructors are responsible that training sticks, &c., are placed in the care of Town Majors and Area Commandants. The wastage of training sticks is unreasonably large.

Be prepared always to give a fighting demonstration of Bayonet work with Superintendent at his lectures.

Go all out with points, parries, and strokes. Finish every stroke with the point of the bayonet a couple of inches from throat of demonstrator. In fact fight him and make yourself a fighting nuisance.

When about to construct a new assault course, go to O.C. and ask that a platoon, under the charge of an Officer (one with pioneering experience if possible), be detailed for the work.

Go beforehand to the ground with the Officer, plan and mark the whole thing out, make sure there are enough tools, and that the timber and necessary stores are available.

If this is done the day before you commence operations, and if the work of digging, etc., is well apportioned and supervised, an average assault course can be completed in one day. If this time-saving proposition is represented rightly to the average C.O. the necessary party will be detailed.

Usually a few fatigue men are allotted from day to day, and the whole business lingers on for weeks.

14.—OUTLINE PROGRAMME OF ASSAULT. — TRAINING FOR A TWELVE DAYS COURSE.

The programme below is intended to be a guide and not a hard and fast proposition. It is arranged to give every student a wide and comprehensive idea of Assault Training in all its phases.

The object of the course is to make an average instructor of each student and not merely a good performer. To secure that end, plenty of class taking must be introduced from the first day.

This programme will be found suitable for Schools and short courses of instruction in Brigades.

First Day.—Counter charge. 1st Exercise. (At dummies on ground or rings.)

Bayonet in attack :—

1. By word of command.
2. By hand indication.
    (To be taught for use only when training sticks are not available.)
3. With training sticks.
4. Quickener in circles of 8 men.
5. At dummies on gallows.

Firing practice: (*a*) Application of fire.

Counter charge. First Exercise.

Second Day.—Counter charge. 1st Exercise.

Bayonet in attack :—(as on 1st day).

Bayonet in defence.

Firing practice :—(*b*) Rapidity and accuracy in alteration of aim and re-loading.

Counter charge. 1st Exercise.

Third Day.—Counter charge. 2nd Exercise.
　　　　Bayonet in attack :—
　　　　　　1.　By hand indication.
　　　　　　2.　With training sticks.
　　　　　　3.　Quickener.
　　　　　　4.　At dummies on gallows and in trenches.
　　　　Bayonet in defence.
　　　　Firing practice :—(c) development of power of
command.
　　　　Counter charge. 2nd Exercise.

Fourth Day.—Counter charge. 3rd Exercise.
　　　　Bayonet in attack :—
　　　　　　1.　With training sticks.
　　　　　　2.　Quickener.
　　　　　　3.　At dummies.
　　　　Bayonet in defence (including butt strokes and
disarms).
　　　　Firing practice :—(d) To train the eye and brain
to work together.

Fifth Day.—Counter charge. 3rd Exercise.
　　　　Bayonet in attack :—
　　　　　　1.　Quickener.
　　　　　　2.　At dummies.
　　　　Bayonet in defence.
　　　　Firing practice :—1.　Application.
　　　　Counter charge. 4th Exercise.

Sixth Day.—Counter charge. 4th Exercise.
　　　　Bayonet in attack, at dummies.
　　　　Bayonet in defence.
　　　　Firing practice :—Simple bayonet and bullet
competitions.
　　　　Preliminary assault with actual firing and scheme
of consolidation.

Seventh Day.—Counter charge. 4th Exercise.
　　　　Bayonet in attack, at dummies.
　　　　Bayonet in defence.
　　　　Final assault over whole course and scheme of
consolidation.

Eighth Day.—Preliminary individual A.T. Competition to find
best men of each section.
　　　　Simple bayonet and bullet competition.

Ninth Day.—Revision of any weak points, as necessary.

Tenth Day.—A.R.A. Competition
Work on improvised Assault and Tin Ring Courses.
Eleventh Day.—Finals of individual A.T. Competition.
Twelfth Day.—Inter-section A.T. Competition.

PART II.—PHYSICAL TRAINING.
15.—THE DAILY LESSON.

Trained Soldiers Table No. 1 is still the foundation of the Daily P.T. Lesson. It should be taught at schools and on other courses of instruction, and should be used also when troops are fit to concentrate sufficiently on the exercises.

There is a tendency to replace entirely or almost entirely the Trained Soldiers Table by Games. This should not be done.

No rule can be made about the right mixture. It is up to the instructor himself to decide how much P.T. proper may be taken, and how much of the games will be necessary to keep the men bright, keen and alert.

Always present the table in a brisk connected manner, with no long boring explanations, and change frequently from one exercise to a game or from one game to another. Be cheery, merry and bright.

Games are an invaluable tonic and have a stimulating effect; especially after some of the more monotonous forms of training. Instructors should preach everywhere that games should be taken for VERY SHORT periods when troops have become stagnant.

The following selection of tabulated games is composed of the most effective games for exercising numbers quickly. (This does not mean that other games may not be given).

If the minds of the men will permit, do a disciplined open out and one or two P.T. exercises, then employ any of the introductory games in the proper sequence.

After having taken a selection of five introductory games, men will be sufficiently stimulated to take a carriage corrective exercise, and a balance exercise. These two cannot satisfactorily be replaced by games. A couple of disciplined exercises sandwiched between games at this stage of lesson, will have a good effect.

After this take the rib, stomach, and back muscles games, putting in a formal body exercise afterwards.

Then take some of the marching, running, and jumping games, concluding always with a formal leg and corrective exercise, a smart form-up and dismiss.

16.—BRAIN STIMULATING TABLE OF GAMES.
INTRODUCTORY.

Leg Exercises.

    1. "O'Grady" Squad drill.

    2. Sitting down cross-legged and standing up with and without turnings (individual competition).

    3. Changing places sideways, backward and forward.

    4. Giants and dwarfs.

    5. Highland Fling.

Neck Exercises.

    1. "O'Grady" variety of usual neck exercises.

Arm Exercises.

    1. "O'Grady" variety of usual arm exercises.

    2. Punching punch pads, or hand punching.

    3. Dead man (in small circles kneeling).

Body Exercises.

    1. F. astr. Passing punch pads up and down ranks sideways.

    2. F. astr. Passing punch pads up and down ranks backward underhand.

    3. F. astr. Passing punch pads up and down ranks backward overhead.

    4. F. astr. Passing punch pads up and down ranks backward through the legs (1, 2, 3 and 4 competitions by ranks).

Leg Exercises.

    1. "Crows and cranes" ranks standing heel to heel, sitting with crossed legs back to back or lying on back head to head, or down on the hands head to head.

    2. Hopping with leg raising sideways.

    3. Astride jumping with arms raising sideways or upward.

    4. Jumping the bag.

    5. Two's and three's.

GENERAL EXERCISES.

Rib Muscles.

    1. F. astr. Throwing punch pads sideways underhand (working in pairs).

    2. F. astr. Throwing punch pads sideways with one hand with bomb throwing action (working in pairs).

    3. Human snake.

Stomach Muscles.

    1. F. astr. Throwing punch pads overhead, backward, with both hands (in pairs).

2. Wheelbarrow race.

3. All fours race.

Back Muscles.

1. F. astr. Throwing punch pads forward, overhead (in pairs).

2. F. astr. Throwing punch pads forward, underhand (in pairs).

3. Putting punch pads with right and left hand (in pairs).

4. Tug of war four to eight aside or in pairs with butchers hook.

5. Cock fighting (in pairs with training sticks under knees).

Marching, Running and Jumping.

1. Crows and cranes.

2. Zig Zag relay race.

3. Relay races, carrying sand bags, punch pads, or with clubs.

4. Hurdling and long jumping over ropes or putties.

5. Human obstacle course, leap frog jump and crawl through legs.

6. Standing jumps competition, forward or backward, one or three jumps.

7. Hop, step and jump.

8. Hopping race.

9. Passing over and under skipping rope.

10. Full knees bend, double march race by ranks.

11. Boat race.

12. Race between ranks, one backward, one forward, and return with caught man by fireman's lift.

13. Ground ball.

14. Hopping in circle, keeping ball in centre, changing feet occasionally.

15. Whip to the gap.

16. Passing rope under squad in two or four ranks.

17. Circle touch ball or punch pad.

18. Bomb ball.

NOTE.—Penalty for " O'Grady " should be frequently changed.

17.—COMPETITION OR DISPLAY.

P.T. TABLE.

Table should be short and attractive, and not take up more than 15 minutes. The simple table given below is merely a guide:

First of all arrange a smart march on, form up and open out; then carry out the following or similar exercises and games.

Leg Exercise.

Jumping the bag (in two or four circles).

Neck Exercise.

Head turning quickly (twice in each direction).

Arm Exercises.

(*a*) A.b. – Arms stretching sideways, forward and upward (twice in each direction).

(*b*) Punching the pad by ranks.

Trunk Exercise.

Ft. astr., as. sidew. str.—Trunk bending sideways quickly.

Leg Exercise.

Hopping with leg raising sideways.

Back Exercise.

H. f. Ft. sidew. pl.—Trunk bending backward.

Balance Exercise.

H. f. Leg raising forward, sideways, and backward (twice each leg).

Rib Muscles.

Ft. astr.—Throwing punch pads sideways underhand (carried out in two or four ranks, each man to have four throws to right and four to left).

Stomach Muscles.

(*a*) On the hands.—Arms bending (twice).

(*b*) From as. b., turn about. As. upw. rais.—Legs raising (twice).

Back Muscles.

Ft. astr., H. f. Trunk bending forward and downward.

Marching, Running and Jumping.

(*a*) H. f. On alternate feet hop (about 12 paces).

(*b*) H. f. With knees raising quick march (about 12 paces).

(*c*) Hurdling over four ropes or putties in fours.

(*d*) Human obstacle race.

(*e*) Upward jumping with turning (twice, once right, once left).

Corrective Exercises.

Arms raising forward and upward, and lowering sideways and downward (three times).

Then re-form ranks. Double March. H. f.

Knees raise as a march out.

NOTE.—In competitions unqualified instructors only should take squads.

18.—P.T. COMPETITION SHEET.

Maximum Marks	March on	L. Ex.	N. Ex.	A. Ex.	Tr. Ex.	L. Ex.	Back Ex.	Rib Ex.	Stomach Ex.	Back Ex.	Hopping	K. Rais. Mch.	Hurdling	Obstacles	Upw. Jump	Cor. Ex.	March out	TOTAL	PLACING
...	10	5	5	10	5	5	5	5	10	5	5	5	5	5	5	5	5		

Judge ....

Date ....

279

19.—GENERAL INSTRUCTIONS.

P.T. parades must be organized for falling in and dismissing as at ALDERSHOT or G.H.Q. School of P. & B.T. If squads are marched from one place to another, correct words of command must be given and march discipline preserved. This is not meant to prevent freedom of movement in games, quickening exercises, &c., or to introduce unnecessary drill into games. But, when taking Table Exercises, insist on perfect steadiness, correct turnings and generally good discipline.

Always run through table with snap. No detailing.

Produce LARGE NUMBERS of punch pads, straffers, jumping ropes and bomb balls; punch pads will serve as medicine bags. All these must be available on ALL P.T. Parades.

Teach everybody the "FIVE MINUTES TABLE." Tell everyone that MULLER or SANDOW would charge £10 for something similar.

PART III.—RECREATIONAL TRAINING.

20.—READ YOUR RECREATIONAL TRAINING PAMPHLET (S.S. 137, MAY, 1918), CAREFULLY.

Remember it is your job to be on Sports Committees to assist and push the organization of games, to see that playing grounds are marked out and that the organization for boxing tournaments is good. Deprecate the running of competitions for the few experts, and foster for all you are worth competitions for the mass.

Advertise the fact that no money prizes may be given and that cups, medals, and silver plated bugles may be obtained through the Superintendents.

Three kinds of competitions are shown below, each arranged on a plan to get large numbers competing in a short time.

1. Short cross-country runs. (Can be run in less than 20 minutes.)

2. Athletic competitions. (Can be run with 4 Platoons of 30 men each in 20 minutes.)

3. Boxing for the mass. (In one hour 120 men should box one 2-minute round.)

21.—CROSS-COUNTRY RUNS.

At the start make pens of screw pickets and wire according to number of teams competing, as per marginal illustration. The same pens will do for the finish.

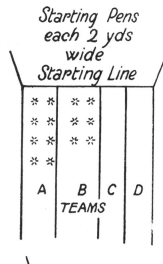

Starting Pens
each 2 yds
wide
Starting Line

A   B C D

TEAMS

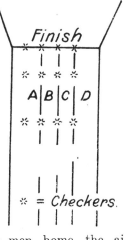

Finish

A B C D

✻ = Checkers

Send men out from pens (1) on a straight out journey to a given point, and back to start; or (2) on a circular route flagged or mapped out. The teams in this case also returning to the same pens they started from.

If possible, arrive at a standard time for course; but where time has not been arrived at by actual practice, send the teams off, and when they come in sight on the way home, the referee should decide on a time allowance, at the expiration of which the pens will be closed. The team with the greatest number in pen at the expiration of time limit wins.

Run the preliminary competition over short distances, i.e., $1\frac{1}{2}$ to $2\frac{1}{2}$ miles, and note condition of men before increasing the distance in future competitions. Maximum distance $3\frac{1}{2}$ to 4 miles.

The officials required are a referee to control the competition and deal with any question arising. and he should be mounted; a starter, a time-keeper, pointsmen to see that men keep the course, and at least two checkers for each pen to count men as they arrive, and pass through pens at finish.

The competitions should be purely team competitions, inter platoon, company, battalion, etc. No special prizes to be given to first men home, the aim being to cultivate and develop collective spirit.

Good runners should be encouraged to coach and advise the men of teams during runs. They should not attempt to race home in front of their respective teams.

With the pens fixed up beforehand a run of $1\frac{1}{4}$ to $1\frac{1}{2}$ miles can easily be completed in fifteen minutes.

This would form a good simple inter-platoon competition.
Officers should take part.

22.—TABLOID ATHLETIC MEETING.

INTER SECTION, SQUAD OR PLATOON ATHLETIC COMPETITIONS FOR
PHYSICAL TRAINING PARADES.

I.—Broad Jump.

Apparatus.—A jumping pit about $11' \times 6'$ with the ground
loosened to a depth of 6 to 8 inches. Mark a take-off at one
end 7' from pit. Place marked pegs along one side of pit every
foot from 7' to 18'.

Competition.—One jump for each man allowed.

Marking.—As each man jumps, the judge jots down the
number of feet jumped. The total number of feet jumped by
section makes up the score for that section. Section with
highest aggregate wins. A man taking off over the mark will
be given one more trial. If he takes off over the mark a second
time, he loses all marks.

II.—High Jump.

Apparatus.—Two poles driven into the ground about 15'
apart, with nails every two inches from $2'$ $6''$ to $4'$ high. A thin
rope or length of tracing tape with weighted bags at the ends.

Competition.—The tape is placed in position at any suitable
height. One jump for each man allowed.

Marking.—Every man clearing the tape (without the
slightest touch), scores one mark for his section. Section with
highest aggregate wins.

III.—Sprint Race.

Apparatus.—Two parallel lines or tapes, long enough for
whole section, 60 to 100 yds. apart. A stop-watch.

Competition and Marking.—The whole section lines up on
one line and sprints to other line.

Time of section is taken from the word " Go " to the last
man of section crossing finish line. The various times place
the sections, and fastest section wins.

IV.—Backward Race.

As for III, but distance 35 to 50 yds., and men run
backwards.

V.—Three Forward Standing Jumps.

Apparatus.—Two parallel lines or tapes 18' to 24' apart.
The standard distance should be carefully worked out to give
the average man a chance of jumping it.

Competition and Marking.—Each man of section who clears the standard distance set, scores 1 mark for his section (4 men can jump at one time). Section with greatest aggregate wins.

VI.—Three Backward Standing Jumps.

As for V, but distance 12 to 16 feet.

NOTE.—One trial jump may be given in all the jumping competitions, before competition proper.

VII.—Inter-Section Relay Race.

Apparatus.—Pens marked as below :—

Front ranks.   Rear ranks.

No. 1 Secn., 6, 5, 4, 3, 2, 1	1, 2, 3, 4, 5, 6. No. 1 Secn.
No. 2 Secn.	No. 2 Secn.
No. 3 Secn.	No. 3 Secn.
No. 4 Secn.	No. 4 Secn.

←— 40 to 80 yds. —→

Four flags or other tokens.

Competition.—No. 1 front rank sprints to No. 1 rear rank and hands flag over to latter. No. 1 rear rank sprints back and hands flag over to No. 2 front rank and so on. Each man in turn comes forward to starting line and after running his distance falls in in rear of team. The last man of rear rank to run holds his flag up on crossing the line and this places the teams.

ORGANIZATION.

Officials.—A Referee to control the moves of sections from one competition ground to another, and give final decision on any point arising.

A Judge for each of the arenas.

A scorer with two blackboards.

The ground should be marked out and jumps prepared by Army Gym. Staff Instructor beforehand.

A good rotation for a Company Competition (Inter-Platoon) is as follows :—

First Series.

No. 1 Platoon   ...   Broad Jump.
No. 2   ,,   High Jump.
No. 3   ,,   ...   Sprints, backward and
                               forward.
No. 4   ,,   ...   Standing Jumps, back
                               and forward.

The Referee should start all these competitions simultaneously by whistle. When first series has been completed, platoons to fall in in two ranks.

For Second series:—

No. 1 Platoon goes to High Jump.

No. 2 Platoon goes to Sprints.

No. 3 Platoon goes to Standing Jumps.

No. 4 Platoon goes to Broad Jump.

and so on until each platoon has taken part in the above six events.

The Relay Race is then run.

After each Series, the referee should cause all the scores to be entered up on one blackboard as below :—

Platoon	Broad Jump	High Jump	3 Forward Jumps	3 B'ward Jumps	Sprint	B'ward Race	Relay Race
No. 1 ...	127						1st
No. 2 ...		18					4th
No. 3 ...			12	13			2nd
No. 4 ...					10½	12½	3rd

On the second blackboard the All Round Championship marks should be shown. These are allotted at the rate of 2 per Platoon competing. With 4 Platoons competing the winner would be allotted 8 marks. The second 6. The third 4 and the last 2 in each competition.

ALL ROUND CHAMPIONSHIP.

Platoon	B.J.	H.J.	3 F.J.	3 B.J.	Sprint	B.R.	Relay	Total	Placing
No. 1 ...	8	2	6	4	4	8	8	40	1st
No. 2 ...	6	8	8	2	2	4	2	32	4th
No. 3 ...	4	6	4	6	6	2	6	34	2nd
No. 4 ...	2	4	2	8	8	6	4	34	3rd

In the event of a tie, the platoon doing best in the Relay will be placed first of tieing teams.

23.—GUIDE TO PLAN OF GROUND FOR TABLOID ATHLETIC MEETING.

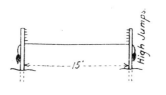

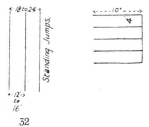

24.—BOXING.

To get the mass boxing requires some enthusiasm from Company Officers, some tact and persistence.

It is no use merely putting the particulars of a competition in Orders, and waiting for things to happen.

The average novice is very shy of starting boxing, but if you can break the ice, and prevent the few known experts from entering into a trial against novices, lots of the latter can be induced to box.

Officers should first of all set things going by boxing for a minute themselves.

Then, if the platoon Officer will fall in his platoon, size the men, get two pairs on the right, and two pairs on the left to put on the gloves, and tell them they are to Box for half a minute in pairs as they stand in the ranks, very few men will refuse.

When arrangements are completed shout "time!" Then the first four pairs will come out of the ranks, shake hands and get busy.

If you can see a man is "getting the knock," call time before the half minute is up. If you discover a man who is obviously too good for the remainder, keep him out of future "breaking-the-ice" bouts.

Whilst the first four pairs are boxing the next four should be putting on the gloves, so that when time is called, the first four fall in, and the second four commence.

When this has been done a few times with a platoon, there will be no difficulty in getting novices to enter for a proper competition.

25.—NOVICES' COMPETITIONS.

It should be the aim at all novices tournaments to get as many Officers, N.C.O.s and men as possible actually to take part. Separate competitions being run for each class.

To run competitions for masses of novices in a short time, the following instructions will be helpful:—

Erect two or three rings 15 foot square with only one rope, anywhere in the open. The bantams can box in one, the feathers in the second, the lights in the third. When these have completed one or two series, the other weights can box.

Instead of boxing three rounds, all pairs box one two minute round for the preliminary series, down to semi-finals. By this method at least twenty bouts per hour can be fought off in each ring. Reserve the semi-finals and finals for a more formal meeting. For these have three one-minute rounds with $\frac{3}{4}$-minute intervals.

The Officials required for each ring are: one Referee, two Judges, one Timekeeper, one M.C., one permanent second in each corner.

Officers must take on the job of refereeing and judging. It is a sporting proposition, and the average Officer can arrive at a just decision in the great majority of cases without any great technical knowledge of the game.

The Army Gymnastic Staff Instructors are trained organizers of boxing tournaments, and should be on the organizing committees.

The Superintendent of P. & B. T. will be also always ready to assist.

26.—HINTS ON CONDUCT OF A FORMAL MEETING.

Officials required.—1 Referee, 2 Judges, 1 Timekeeper, 1 M.C., 1 Register Keeper, 1 Dressing-room Steward, 2 or 3 Dressers, 4 Seconds, 2 Judges' Orderlies, 1 Steward's Orderly. Except the Referee, Judges and Timekeeper (who shall be Officers) all will be under the M.C.

Kit required.—1 ring, 4 sets of gloves, 1 blackboard (when inter-unit competition is in progress), 6 towels, 2 sponges, 2 basins, 2 stools, 2 bottles, 2 tea cans for clean water, 2 boxes of sawdust, 2 red and 2 green sashes for competitors, 1 stop-watch, 1 pound of resin, 4 chairs, 2 small tables for judges and 1 for referee and timekeeper, 1 whistle for referee, 1 red and green flag by which referee announces his decision, books A.B. 153B, and pencils for referee and judges.

Ring.—Ring, 14 ft. to 18 ft. square, with 2 ft. margin outside ropes. Top rope 4 ft. high. Floor should be covered. Posts, if flush with ropes, to be padded. One post draped red, post diagonally opposite green.

Organization.—If possible an enclosure for Officers and one for W.O.s and N.C.O.s should be arranged for around ring. A clear passage way to be preserved from dressing room, and 2 seats reserved at ring side for next pair of competitors, the following two competitors should be ready in the dressing room with gloves on. First named of each pair should always occupy the same corner and wear the colour of that corner.

The salient points of the I.S.B.A. Rules should be explained to competitors beforehand, and the principal differences between N.S.C. and I.S.B.A. Rules explained to onlookers.

Where the spectators become noisy during bouts, an appeal by M.C. or Referee will generally be effective. A few N.C.O.s judiciously distributed among the onlookers will help to preserve order.

Weighing.—Competitors should assemble at a specified time and fall in according to the weights at which they have entered, Bantamweights leading, Featherweights next, and so on. The scales should be set at Bantamweight (*see* table below), and the men step on in rotation. If a man does not turn the scale his entry as a Bantamweight is accepted. If he is above the weight he has the option of falling in with the Featherweights and being weighed in that class. By this method 4 or 5 men per minute can be weighed. If competitors are weighed fully dressed without equipment an addition of 13 lbs. (or 6 kilos) must be made for clothes.

Weights.	English and Colonial.	French equivalent.
Heavy ...	Catch	Catch
Light Heavy ...	12 st. 7 lbs. (175 lbs.) and under	80 kilos.
Middle ...	11 ,, 6 ,, (160 ,,) ,, ,,	73 ,,
Welter ...	10 ,, 7 ,, (147 ,,) ,, ,,	67 ,,
Light ...	9 ,, 9 ,, (135 ,,) ,, ,,	61 ,,
Feather ...	9 ,, 0 ,, (126 ,,) ,, ,,	57 ,,
Bantam ...	8 ,, 6 ,, (118 ,,) ,, ,,	53 ,,

Drawing Rounds.—The number of entries in a competition, if not already a power of 2, *i.e.*, 4, 8, 16, etc., should be made so by means of byes. If there are ten entries there must be 6 byes and 2 fights in order to bring the total to 8 competitors for the next series.

Number of Byes.—All byes must be in the first series. By deducting the number of competitors from the power of 2 immediately above, the number of byes is arrived at. By deducting the power of 2 immediately below from the number of competitors, the number of fights is found, *i.e.* 11 competitors from 16 give 5 byes ; or 8 deducted from 11 competitors give 3 fights. Byes should not be fought.

Order of Fighting.—With 11 competitors the first 6 drawn out of the hat will fight, first versus second, third versus fourth, fifth versus sixth. The remaining 5 will have byes in the order in which they are drawn. There will be no further drawing.

The winner of first bout will fight winner of second and so on
in each series.

Example of Draw.—

	1st Series.	2nd Series.	Semi-final.	Final.	Winner.
1	Black	} Brown			
2	Brown		} Jones		
3	Smith	} Jones		} Jones	
4	Jones				
5	Robinson	} Harvey			
6	Harvey		} Harvey		} Jones
Byes .					
7	Nichols	Nichols			
8	Mappin	Mappin	} Webb		
9	Webb	Webb		} Webb	
10	Roberts	Roberts	} Roberts		
11	Inman	Inman			

*Arrangements of Programme.—*The programme should be
so arranged and numbered that men are not asked to fight too
frequently in one day or with too short an interval between the
bouts.

*Duration of Meeting.—*The number of bouts in a competition
is always one below the number of entries. In calculating
prospective duration of meeting allow 9 minutes for each bout
of 3 two-minute rounds. In case of large entries, preliminary
series up to semi-finals should be one round of 2 minutes.

*Prizes.—*Money prizes must not be given. All meetings
must be held under the I.S.B.A. Rules. The following G.R.O.
on the subject was published on January 7th, 1917.

> *2059.—Boxing.*
>
> 1. All boxing competitions and contests must be
> carried out under the R.N. & A.B.A. Rules, copies of
> which can be obtained from O. i/c. E.F.C. (Northern),
> G.H.Q., 2nd Echelon ; price 9d.
>
> 2. No money prizes may be given.
>
> 3. To cover the expenses of the meeting, *e.g.*,
> hiring of hall, lighting, etc., a small fee may be charged,
> but this fee should be fixed at such an amount that
> the total received should not exceed, if possible, the
> estimated cost of above. On all such occasions a balance
> sheet will be kept and forwarded to Headquarters,
> P. & B.T., B.A.F., with profits, if any.

NOTE.—I.S.B.A. Rules have been published since and
govern Services competitions.

Marking, etc.—Instructions in marking and information *re* prizes will be found in S.S. 137 (*Revised Edition May, 1918*), paras. 38 to 49a and appendix.

27.—SALIENT POINTS OF I.S.B.A. RULES.

1. *Stop bout to check.*—When it is necessary to check a boxer, the bout is first stopped, then the referee checks one or both boxers.

2. *Holding.*—Holding in any way is not allowed.

3. *Punching and holding.*—Punching when holding is not allowed, but if one man only is holding, the other is quite in order to punch.

4. *Break away.*—This term is not used as either one or both men are holding ; the bout should be stopped and one or both checked.

5. *Silent count.*—When a man is knocked down, time is counted silently.

6. *Knock down.*—A man who has knocked his opponent down must stand right away from him and wait for the referee's order to " box on."

All the above rules have been framed for the protection of the clean sporting boxer.

RECREATIONAL TRAINING.

28.—HINTS ON ORGANIZATION OF ATHLETIC MEETINGS

Personnel.—1 Referee, 3 Judges (more where various competitions are held simultaneously), 1 Starter, 1 Timekeeper, 2 Lap Scorers, 1 Groundman, 2 Measurers, 1 Marshal, 1 Clerk of Course, 1 Dressing-room Steward, 1 Assistant Dressing-room Steward, 1 Recorder, 1 Judge's Orderly, 1 Dressing-room Steward's Orderly, 1 Recorder's Orderly, 2 Blackboard Orderlies.

Duties.—REFEREE.   To decide all points of law, and to act with Judges as appeals committee.

JUDGES.   To judge all events and to take cognisance of fouls.

STARTER.   To start all track events.

TIMEKEEPER.   To time track events, especially where fastest losers run in final.

MARSHAL.   To receive competitors from Dressing-room Steward and assemble them at starting point ; to draw heats and positions.

CLERK OF COURSE. To announce events and results, and to call names or numbers in field events.

D.R. STEWARD. To assemble competitors at dressing room and to turn them out one event in advance.

RECORDER. To keep records of all events and marks for inter-unit trophy, and to prepare prize list.

GROUNDMAN. To have charge of all material.

JUDGE'S ORDERLY. To take results and convey to recorder, and to prepare second round, etc., heats for starter.

BLACKBOARD ORDERLIES. To post results and unit marks.

Material.—Whitewash and brush, flags or substitutes for marking track, 1 measuring tape, 1 rifle or pistol with ammunition, 1 hank of white worsted, 1 bell, 2 blackboards (1 for results, 1 for unit scores), 4 to 6 picket posts for finishes on straight and lap tracks, 4 to 6 flags for relay race, breast numbers when warranted by entries, numbers or balls for drawing positions, 1 stop-watch, 1 shot or hammer, numbered pegs to extent of entries for shot or hammer, 1 pair jumping standards with sufficient laths or tracing tape, 1 take-off board for long jump, 2 pieces of scantling 11 ft. long marked in feet and inches for long jump, 1 rake, recorder's books, postcards or equivalents for judge's orderly, 1 megaphone for C. of C., hurdles when needed.

Lap Track.—Following measurements give 440 yards tracks measured 1 ft. outside the lines.

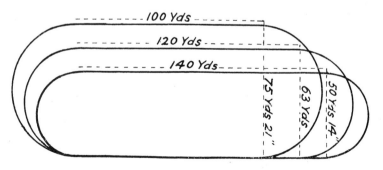

Organization.—Make ground as brilliant as circumstances permit. Have band in attendance. Arrange impressive prize distribution. Separate enclosures for Officers and for N.C.O.s. Provide tea on ground, especially in men's enclosure. Avoid the slightest delay between events. Men should not be asked to compete in consecutive events. This can be avoided by alternating long distance with short distance and field events. The Relay is the hardest race to fit in, as it engages sprinters, middle distance and long distance runners.

Humorous events can be interspersed among standard competitions. (For standard competitions, *see* para. 57—S.S. 137, May, 1918 Ed.).

Duration of Meeting.—Allot a specified time to each event, and adhere strictly to it. The following time allowances will serve as a guide to compilation of programme :—

100 Yards	...	3 heats per minute.
440 Yards	...	1 heat per 1½ minutes.
120 Yards Hurdles ...	...	2 heats per minute.
880 Yards	...	1 heat per 3½ minutes.
Mile	...	1 heat per 6 minutes.
Mile Relay	...	1 heat per 7 minutes.
High Jump	...	45 seconds per competitor.
Long Jump, Shot and Hammer	...	30 seconds per competitor.

Important Officials.—Dressing-room Steward and Marshal. With them lies responsibility for keeping programme up to time.

Only the most energetic and resourceful N.C.O.s should be given these jobs.

Starting.—Stand behind the competitors, and fire immediately the men are steady. Fire above head where time is being taken.

Caution.—"On your marks," "Set," " Fire." No competitor shall touch the ground in front of his mark with any portion of his body. Starter may penalise at discretion for getting over mark :—

1ST OFFENCE :	For races up to 220 yards	...	1 yard.
	Between 220 and 440 yards	...	2 yards.
	Between 440 and 880 yards	...	3 yards.
	Over 880 yards	... ...	5 yards.
2ND OFFENCE :	Similar penalties.		
3RD OFFENCE :	Disqualification.		

Judging.—A stake or picket post should be driven on each side of finish, at least 1 yard clear of track. Drive a nail perpendicularly into tops of stakes and stretch worsted from nail to nail. Judges sight over nails and can determine difference of an inch between competitors.

General Instructions.—100 yards maximum number per heat 8; 3 ft. frontage for each competitor.

Ten is a comfortable number to start for 440 yards, 16 for 880 yards, and 30 for a mile, but these numbers may be exceeded in order to avoid running preliminary heats. Eight teams, too, can be run from one start for relay race, for same reason, although four is the ideal number.

Mile Relay	...	Two 220's, 440, and 880 yards. Track should be marked 10 yards behind both 220 starts for taking over flag. Competitors taking over outside those marks disqualified.
120 yards Hurdles		10 flights hurdles, 2 ft. 6 in. to 3 ft. 6 in. 15 yards from start to first hurdle, same from last hurdle to finish, 10 yards between hurdles; maximum 6 per heat.
High Jump	...	If laths not available use tracing-tape and sandbags, 3 jumps at each height. Displacing bar or touching tape counts a jump.
Long Jump	...	Take-off board 5 in. wide, whitened and sunk flush with ground. Measure from front of take-off to rearmost heelmark. Crossing take-off counts a try.
Shot ...	...	16-lb. shot, 3 puts from 7-ft. circle or square. Measure from front of circle to first pitch of shot. Crossing scratch counts a try.
Hammer ...	...	16-lb. haft, not more than 4 ft. Measure as for shot, 3 throws.
Cricket Ball	...	3 throws. Measure from first pitch of ball to scratch line or that line produced. Thrower shall not cross scratch in delivering ball.

NOTE.—In Long Jump, Shot and Hammer, best 3 competitors, after first trial, are each allowed 3 further tries.

29.—PLATOON OBSTACLE RACE.

The rules for Platoon Obstacle Race and guide plan of course may be of help to organizers of Athletic Meetings. The former are framed for an inter-platoon competition, a competition of this description being of greater value than an individual one.

Conditions.—The platoon will form up " in fours " behind starting line in fighting kit.

At " go " the platoon will start to surmount each obstacle in turn, by fours; the whole of the platoon must surmount the first obstacle before proceding to the second one, and so on right round the course.

After surmounting the last obstacle the whole of the platoon will form up after crossing the original starting line.

Time will be taken when the last man of the platoon crosses the line.

Marking.—The time of each platoon will be taken and the platoon completing the course in the fastest time will score 100 marks. The other teams will have 10 marks deducted from the maximum (100 marks) for each 10 seconds or part of 10 seconds over the fastest team's time.

One judge will be posted at each obstacle, and will judge the style and method of surmounting the obstacle.

A maximum of 10 marks will be allowed for each obstacle.

For every man failing to complete course 10 marks will be deducted.

Officials.—(1) A referee to see that the conditions are observed and to deal with any question arising.

(2) A starter and timekeeper.

(3) One judge at each obstacle.

(4) A scorer.

30.—GUIDE PLAN AND DIAGRAMS OF OBSTACLE COURSE FOR ATHLETIC MEETINGS, &c.

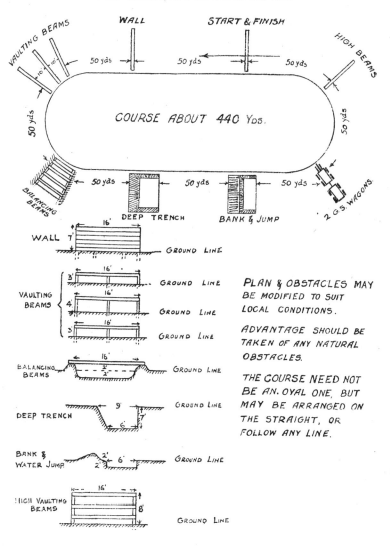

PLAN & OBSTACLES MAY BE MODIFIED TO SUIT LOCAL CONDITIONS.

ADVANTAGE SHOULD BE TAKEN OF ANY NATURAL OBSTACLES.

THE COURSE NEED NOT BE AN OVAL ONE, BUT MAY BE ARRANGED ON THE STRAIGHT, OR FOLLOW ANY LINE.

31.—ALL-ROUND CHAMPIONSHIP.

Whenever a series of competitions are held a scheme of marking to discover the best all round section, squad or platoon should be prepared. If a challenge trophy can be provided it will help, but an honours board will be found sufficient.

Technical training competitions should be inter-mixed with Recreational Training competitions as this gives a fillip all round to work and play.

The following systems of marking for separate competitions and for all-round championships will be found useful.

1.—For Separate Competitions.

Marks should be awarded according to "Recreational Training," S.S. 137, May, 1918, and as below:—

Major Events.

Competition.

Team Assault Training	...	Paras. 33 and 34
Boxing ...	...	„ 46, 47 and 48
Cross-country running	...	„ 67
Wrestling ...	...	„ 80, 81 and 82

Football ⎱ Winning team in each match 2 marks
Tug-of-War ⎰ for its unit.
Hockey ⎰ Losing team 1 mark.

Minor Events.

Individual Assault Training   Paras. 23, 24 and 28
Medicine bag Badminton ⎫
Rope Quoit   „ ⎪   Winning team in each match
Bomb Ball   ⎬   2 marks for its unit.
Basket Ball ·   ⎪   Losing team 1 mark.
Rounders   ⎭

2.—For All-round Championship.

Championship marks are allotted in "Major Events" at the rate of 2, and in "Minor Events" at the rate of 1 for each competing team or unit.

Example:—4 units competing.

(*a*) Major Events:—Winning team or unit 8; second 6; third 4; and fourth 2 marks.

(*b*) Minor Events:—Winning team or unit 4; second 3; third 2; and fourth 1 marks.

All-round Championship Table for a Company.

Platoon	MAJOR EVENTS.							MINOR EVENTS						Total Marks	Placing
	Team Assault Training	Boxing	Cross-country Running	Wrestling	Football	Tug-of-War	Hockey	Individual Assault Training	Medicine bag Badminton	Rope Quoit Badminton	Bomb Ball	Basket Balls	Rounders		
No. 1	6	6	6	4	6	6	6	3	2	3	3	2	3	56	1st
,, 2	8	4	4	8	8	4	4	2	1	2	1	3	2	51	2nd
,, 3	2	8	8	2	2	2	2	4	4	1	2	1	4	38	4th
,, 4	4	2	2	6	4	8	8	1	3	4	4	4	1	51	3rd

No. 1 Platoon did not win a single competition, but showed best all-round efficiency and so won championship.

Nos. 2 and 4 tied, but the former gained 40 marks in Major Events against 34 gained by No. 4 and so took priority.

PART IV.—SPECIAL TIPS TO INSTRUCTORS.
32.—WHAT TO DO AND WHAT NOT TO DO.

1. An A.G.S. Instructor is expected to be full of resource, initiative and energy ; to be continually at work even when no classes are training. There is always something to do on an assault course in the way of repairs, improvements, etc. In spare time, punch pads, straffers, bomb balls, etc., must be made.

2. Don't detail ; don't talk. Give men lots of practice and give tips whilst they are practising. Be cheery when instructing. Don't forget to encourage.

3. Half-hour lessons, going full speed ahead, are the best.

4. Instructors with brigades should ask for small classes when brigades are in the line, ~~say 2 Officers, 4 N.C.O.s and 6 privates likely to become N.C.O.s~~ *of platoon of* On all Brigade courses of instruction run a scheme of inter-regimental competitions right through the course. This should include as many competitions as possible, such as boxing, wrestling, cross-country runs, football, etc., as well as assault training. A guide to marking for an all-round championship is shown in this pamphlet.

Officers and N.C.O.s who have taken part in such a scheme whilst on a course will probably become keen to reproduce the organization in their respective units.

5. Report any interesting bayonet work you hear of.

6. Get Officers to take part in the trainings or at least to assist in judging, directing, etc.

7. Show the various instructions and plans to Officers and N.C.O.s who are interested.

8. Keep a pocket book on your person for Superintendent's remarks.

9. Weekly returns are not required, but report at once when short of training kit, when not fully employed, or when in any difficulties. Report to Superintendent by wire whenever you are moved. Letters to be addressed " Superintendent " and not by name.

Always correspond with the Superintendent, never directly with the Deputy-Inspector.

10. Be an example of smartness, and salute only in the proper manner, with no extra quiffs and twiddles of the hands.

11. All C.S.M.s and a/C.S.M.s must wear crossed swords and crowns on both cuffs of tunic, small crossed swords and crowns on shoulder straps and large crossed swords and crowns as cap badges.

All these must be of polished metal. On overcoats the worsted crown only is to be worn.

Red and black jerseys may only be worn by Staff Instructors and Instructors attached to the A.G. Staff.

Be loyal in letter and spirit to the Department at home and overseas.

33.—MATERIALS AND SOURCES OF SUPPLY.

The Superintendent can supply :—

> Parry sticks.
> Boche faces and figures.

He may be able to supply in emergencies small quantities of the following stores :—

> Bayonet sacks.
> Twine, sail.
> Needles, collar packing.
> Discs.
> Boxing, ring rope.
> Jumping ropes.
> Wire clips for blank targets.
> The loan of tin ring cutters.

The R.E. will supply :—

> Gallows material.
> Sandbags.
> Wire.
> Revetting material.

The Ordnance will supply, on requisition on A.F.G.994 in duplicate:—

    Twine, sail.

    Needles, collar packing.

(Attach covering letter to indents stating that these stores are necessary for training).

    Sacks, bayonet fighting.

(Authority: G.H.Q., Letter O.B.1211, dated 16-6-16).

    Rope (including tug-of-war ropes on loan).

(Authority: G.H.Q., Letter O.S.A.2/733, dated 5-8-17).

    *Red and black jerseys.

    *Blue serge trousers.

    *Shoes, gymnasia.

    *Belts, gymnasia.

(Authority: G.R.O. 2853, dated 22-11-17).

The A.S.C. will supply straw or damaged hay for filling sacks at the rate of 20 lbs. per sack.

(Authority: G.H.Q., Letter O.B.1211, dated 16-6-16).

The Publications Department, Army Printing and Stationery Services, Boulogne, will supply on indent:—

    Discs, bayonet fighting.

34.—PAMPHLETS.

Assault Training—Septr. 1917. S.S. 185. 40/W.O./4063.

Recreational Training—(revised edition). S.S. 137. May 1918.

A.R.A. Platoon Competition. O B./1618/D.

Supplementary Tables, Physical Training, 1916.

With Games, 1917. 40/W.O./4056.

35.—DEMONSTRATIONS.

Whenever you can get a class to give a demonstration, do so. The programme given below is a guide, and will make a good show; but it can be simplified, shortened or amended according to the capabilities of the class.

Demonstrations should not last more than one hour. Somebody should act as showman.

36.—DEMONSTRATION OF ASSAULT AND PHYSICAL TRAINING GAMES.

(i.) Complete Assault Training Lesson when only training sticks are available. (10 minutes).

    1. Counter charge, "first exercise" (at dummies on ground or at rings).

---

*Indents in the first place to be sent to Superintendent for approval of issue.

2. Bayonet in attack.
    (*a*) Pointing by word of command (one rank).
    (*b*)   ,,   by hand indication (one rank).
    To be taught for use only when training sticks are not available.
    (*c*) Pointing by training sticks (one rank).
    (*d*) Quickening practice in circles facing outward.
3. Firing practice (*d*) page 7 of Assault Training, which includes Counter charge " fourth exercise."

(ii.) Complete Assault Training Lesson where Assault Course is available. (20 minutes),
    1. Counter charge " third exercise."
    2. Bayonet in attack (at gallows).
        (*a*) Long point at kidneys at a walk from " on guard."
        (*b*) Long and Short points at a run from " on guard."
        (*c*) Long point and jab at the charge from " the rest."
        (*d*) Long and short point and jab, at the charge from " the rest."
    3. Bayonet in defence.
        (*a*) Parrying from " on guard " (one rank).
        (*b*) Parrying from " short point positions " (one rank).
        (*e*) Parrying from " jab position " (one rank).
        (*d*) Butt strokes (one rank).
        (*e*) Disarms (one rank).
    4. Preliminary Assault from Centre Trench. firing at disappearing targets, posting of sentries and consolidating.

(iii.) Brain stimulating tabulated games and exercises. (25 minutes).

Introductovy Exercises.

    1. L. Ex. Jumping the bag.
    2. N. Ex. O'Grady (variety of exercises).
    3. A. Ex. Punching sand bags suspended on wire, bayonet dummies, or punch pads.
    4. Tr. Ex. Passing bag sideways (competition by ranks).
    5. L. Ex. Crows and cranes (from various positions).

General Exercises.
Exercises for the muscles of the body.
Formal.—
    1. Formal Back Ex. H.F. Ft. Sidw. Pl. trunk bending backward.

2. Control Ex. H.F. Leg raising forward, sideways and backward.

3. Rib Muscles. Throwing punch pads sideways underhand.

4. Stomach Muscles. Throwing punch pads overhead backward.

5. Back Muscles. Throwing punch pads forward underhand, forward overhead and putting with right and left hands.

N.B.—These last three exercises to be carried out in two ranks about eight paces apart, and about three paces between men of each rank. Every man to throw the bag four times in each style.

Running and Jumping Exercises.

1. Relay Race (fetching and carrying medicine bag).
2. Hurdling over several ropes in fours.
3. Human obstacle race.
4. Boat race.

Final Exercises.

1. Leg. Ex. H.F. Heels raising and knees bending.
2. Corr. Ex. arms raising sideways and upward.

37.—ASSAULT TRAINING COMPETITIONS.

1. Simple bullet and bayonet competition.

Four sections of four men to demonstrate each competition separately. Then the same four sections to demonstrate the four competitions being run simultaneously with one " change rounds."

2. Individual Competitions.

Four men taking part in the competition, to illustrate every phase of it, *i.e.*, (*a*) The points and jab, butt strokes, one disarm. (*b*) Tin ring course. (*c*) Individual Assault, firing three rounds blank at start, and five live rounds at range. The other men of demonstrating party to act as judges, scorer, timekeeper, and to replace tin rings or discs. In fact the whole organization should be shown.

3. Team Competition over Assault Course.

Two small teams to compete. Remainder of class to judge, score, etc.

4. A.R.A. Competitions.

Can be demonstrated on short range firing blank at first fire position, with one section.

9

The Value of Games in Training for War

Games were recognised as enhancing the fighting spirit in the soldier prior to the First World War and experience gained during the war confirmed this. In 1931, General Harington declared in the preface of *Games and Sports in the Army*, a handbook published by the Army Sports Control Board, that the war had been won by the leather in the shape of footballs and boxing gloves. In doing so he was expressing official recognition of the military value of sports and games.[1] This same sentiment is conveyed in the following lecture by Lt Col R. B. Campbell, who, following his service as Deputy Inspector of Physical & Bayonet Training in France, became Inspector of Physical Training from 1918 to 1923.

*

Value of Games in Training for War
By
Col. R. B. Campbell – Inspector PT

23-01-1922

1. The Magnitude of our Achievement.

We don't know what we owe to our games in winning this War.
I will try and make you.
Let us reverse the conditions of the War.

Supposing the Bosche, at the outbreak of War, had only seven divisions to put in the Field and the French with their 120 Divisions to support them. No high explosive shells; no big guns; very little ammunition even for the small guns; only two machine guns to a battalion' very few aeroplanes and no aeroplane liaison with the Troops. His people scattered all over the world, technically untrained and prejudiced against any form of Military Training.

On the other hand suppose we had what the Bosche started with. Over two hundred fighting divisions made up of the flower of the British Empire, trained and organised with concentrated energy of the nation of three big campaigns. Ready to start off the mark at the 'crack of the pistol' equipped with huge guns with an abundant supply of high explosive ammunition, a highly organized air service, and machine guns in quantity. In fact everything which the thought and energy of an ambitious nation could invent. No trenches or organized defence to bar the way! How long would the war have lasted? Not many weeks. Yet in spite of these overwhelming odds we beat the Bosche!! We must have some great national advantage over him to have been able to do this, otherwise organization, backed by technical training, is valueless.

2. Our National Asset.

People said we did it with an untrained Army! An impossibility. Since we have been children we have been training for War, and on the best possible lines, by means of our National Games. The nearest approach to a ready made soldier is a man good at our British fighting games - Football, Cricket, Boxing - trained by means of games and play.

3. Nature's method of Training.

The natural way to train is the way that nature trains. How does a tigress train her cubs to fight and hunt? By mimic fights and mimic hunts in the form of games. How does a Kitten develop its qualities which enable it to catch a mouse or bird? By play. How do puppies learn to fight? By fighting in play. We have all seen this, times out of number. They are trained without realizing; they love their training. You can't stop a tiger cub, kitten or puppy from playing. Their Nature compels them to play games. It is the best and most natural means of teaching.

4. British Games

It is the same with our British Games and pastimes of Football, Cricket, Boxing etc., etc. Each one of these Games is a mimic battle and develops those qualities that are required for War. The training for each should go hand in hand.

5. Qualities Required in War

What are the qualities we require for War? First, Physical Fitness. What is Physical Fitness? It is a combination of good health, good nerve and endurance. It is the foundation on which you build up the spirit. It is the foundation of moral. You can't have moral in an unfit man. I ask you Athletes here. What is the first thing you do when you train for any vigorous game? You get physically fit. Can you play a Game of rugby if you are unfit? You know you can't. Not only can you not play but you are a handicap to your side. Can an unfit man box or play cricket? All of you have seen many a good record gone, just because a man neglected to get fit before he took part in a game or competition. Technical knowledge or experience is of very little use in an unfit man.

i) Physical fitness

If you think about it you will realize that from 70 to 80 per cent of your training for games is concentrated on getting fit! You realize this in a thing you continually practice and thoroughly understand. Now what about War? Is an unfit man any good? No! He depresses you; he has no reserve force; he fills the ambulances; he is a moral killer. He is just as big a handicap to his side as an unfit man is in a game of rugby. He is better out of it. You know this, you have seen it time and again. But it is the obvious point which is lost sight of. You see the first principles of War and Games are the same. Fitness.

ii) Resources

What is the next quality we want in War? Think what you did when you went over the top? Every man had a job to do - you, Lewis gunners, you Bombers, you Riflemen - every man had to think and act for himself. Call this what you like - executive or initiative abilities. It is the brain and muscle working together and being able to act on the spur of the moment. It is resource.

What makes a man good at games? Making an opening and taking advantage of it. Seeing an opening and acting at once. You see this in any game. Take a game of Cricket; a man fielding; the ball is hit, the batsman commence to run, the fielder snaps up the ball. Does he blindly throw, sees which batsman is furthest from the wickets, and throws it accordingly to the bowler or wicket-keeper! It is the action of a second. The very qualities we want in a modern soldier. It is the same in other games. It is developed in all games. I will agree so. You know this. The Training for War and Games is harmonious.

iii. The Fighting Spirit.

What is the next quality you want in your man? What compels a man in war? The fighting spirit. Without it, the fittest and best trained man is useless. Now what do we mean by the 'fighting spirit?' It is not dashing 'over the top'; it is 'sticking it'. Sticking the hardships of War, the exposure, the weather, the discomforts. Being cheery when things look blue, when you hear bad news, when you are tired. Sticking it, after a reverse. Sticking it when you are wounded. Sticking it instead of going sick. Sticking it in the half-filled shell holes after the Somme. The Bosche could not; he lacked the fighting spirit and went back. Sticking it like we stuck it after Mons; during the Bosche offensive in 1918. You fellows know this, nobody better than you, for I speak in the concrete to you.

Let us see how this spirit is inculcated and developed by our Games. If you get a punch in a Boxing Bout, what do you do? Clench you teeth, hide your feeling from your opponent and hit back. This is the fighting spirit. Every punch you get, every bout you fight develops. If you are hurt at footer, what do you do? Lie down and whimper? Not a bit of it. You stick it and don't give way to pain. Unconsciously you are developing your spirit and character. If at half-time the other side leads, what do you do in the second half? Play all the harder. That is the fighting spirit - the unconquerable spirit - the unconquerable spirit of the Briton which Napoleon admitted beat him at Waterloo! A spirit which has taken centuries to develop can't be broken by one War.

iv) Discipline

What is another essential quality for War Discipline? Discipline is not physical. It is mental. It is obtained by training the mind.

We know of two kinds of discipline. Discipline by fear - which is Bosche, and discipline by interest, which is British. What does the Bosche say? To make a man break a man, break his spirit. That is why they lost this war. What is our Motto? Raise a man's moral, develop his spirit. It is the spirit of discipline that we want, that unconquerable spirit of Casablanca.

A platoon goes over the top. Every man will go over, that is no criterion of discipline, for it a man doesn't he will be shot. The platoon advances, the men scatter, each is 'on his own'. Now comes the Test! Will each man play the game, with nobody to compel him and to punish him if he scrimshank's and hides in a shell hole? Will he play the Game behind his Commander's back? That is the test of true discipline; self-discipline' the spirit of discipline; the spirit which inspires self-effort.

Now is this spirit developed by our games what do you Boxers do when you train? You work on your own, in the Gym, on the Road. You keep it up day after day, you give up your leisure to do it. You discipline yourselves. This is self-discipline; the spirit of self-effort.

Watch a game of footer; each man is in his place; he keeps it because he knows it is the game; his mind is disciplined to it. The outside right gets the ball near his own goal - watch him! He takes it down the touch line. He nears the opponent's goal. Does he try and shoot a goal himself? No! It is not the game. Discipline tells him he must centre it. Discipline tells him that the centre-forward will be in his place. He doesn't hesitate, he centres. The centre-forward gets the ball and shoots a goal. The centre gets the applause of the spectators; gets the notice in the papers. But it was the outside right who did the work. But he played the game. This team discipline - without it a side is useless. It is discipline by interest, the true discipline of battle and of our games.

You are in the Long Field, playing cricket. For over half-an hour no ball has come near you. But every time the bowler bowls you make a mental effort to get on your toes ready to start off at once to save a boundary or hold a catch, in case the ball does come. There is nobody there to see whether you do it or not, but you do it all the same. You play the game. Every time you make that mental effort you are performing an act of self-discipline. You are training and disciplining your brain. You see it, now, don't you. Discipline is training of the mind. Increase the mentality and you will increase and develop discipline. It is the only true discipline. I know of no better way of developing this spirit of discipline than by means of British games, played in the spirit of true sport.

v) Self- Sacrifice.

One more quality we must have. The greatest quality of all. What do we give the highest reward for? What do we give the V.C. for? Self-sacrifice. If you want to be a good boxer, what do you do? Practice boxing don't you. It you want to be a good footballer, what do you do? Practice football. The more you practice the better you become. So it is with any quality you want to develop in yourself or in your men. <u>You must perform acts of that quality.</u> You can become a fine character just the same as you can become a fine cricketer. You realize this in your games, for it is concrete, you see the result of your efforts. Let us talk in the concrete and see how self-sacrifice is developed by our Games. Take a game of Footer. A man comes charging down with the ball, you must tackle him- do you hesitate? No! you don't consider his size or whether you will get hurt, you 'wash out' self and think only of the side. You tackle him, perhaps you get knocked over or kicked, that's nothing. You have performed an act of self-sacrifice.

A mass of burly rugby forwards come down the field with the ball at their feet. What does the little 'half' do? Without hesitating, he throws himself on the ball. A fine act. It even inspires the crowd - they cheer - the whole game is made up of similar acts. They may be only small acts, but it is the continued performance of these small acts which develops the character and enables one to perform the big acts.

Every player will leave the field a bigger man than when he came on. Then there is boxing. Who has seen the Public schools Championships? The Army Championships? What is the motive of the Boxers? To fight for their side. To get 'hammered' for their side, for remember there is only one winner in a competition. The spirit of the boxers inspires the audience, for spirit is catching.

I was refereeing the Boxing Competition at the 2nd Army School at Wisques in France. There was no prize for the team which scored the most points. The points were two for the winner of a bout, one for the loser, if he did not give in, and an extra half-point for a especially plucky loser.

There was one bout I remember well. One of the competitors was a champion boxer, his opponent was a novice. One the call of time, the novice dashed up at the champion and tried to 'mix it up', it was his only chance. A punch on the jaw put him 'down'. He was up in a second and at his opponent again. Another on the jaw sent him down for some few seconds. But he struggled up again and fought with the utmost gallantry. A third time he was floored, after about eight seconds he recovered his senses and endeavoured to struggle to his feet and continue the fight. He remonstrated when I stopped the fight. I awarded him an extra half point for his gallantry. There was a storm of applause. Who was it for? Not the winner, but that game loser. What had he done? Not only had he won a half point for his side, but he had inspired and thrilled that audience. That is why he got the ovation of the meeting. When you hear a band play a stirring march; it thrills you and brings out the best in you, doesn't it? But it is nothing to how you are thrilled and inspired when you see such an exhibition of pluck and self-sacrifice as that novice gave, in the Boxing Ring. It is a picture that everyone in that packed hall took away with him., a picture indelibly impressed on the mind.

Such examples you will see at the Public Schools Championships and the Army Championships. You will see the spirit of one lad stir and enthuse a packed house of thousands, and in every man in that house will feel the better man for the inspiration.

6. National System of Training

Every word I said, you know is true, for I speak to you in the concrete. You have seen these things and you understand the games just as well as I do. What I am talking about is not a 'one man's show' – 'somebody's invention' it is the national inheritance of every Briton. It is the British System of Physical and Moral development, the finest and most practical in the World. It is a part of our National Temperament. It is in our blood. Games are a part of our life, the part we like best, and have made us what we are. They must be regarded as our most cherished possession. We must make full use of this love for manly games.

Perhaps you do not realize the brain value of this. If you do a thing you like you are interested in it; interest is the fundamental principle of all training. Interest means that your brain is stimulated your body must be stimulated. Your whole outlook of life depends on your mind. I will give you a concrete example. you are in the field for six days and nights; it has rained. You get more and more depressed. You catch yourself saying 'what is the good of it all'. The fight seems to ooze out of you and you feel like chucking it. The weather changes, there is not a cloud in the sky. You feel bucked up, and say to yourself you feel twice the man you did yesterday. You are the same fellow as you were yesterday, but the sunshine brightens your brain, which in turn bucks up your body. Bear in mind the value of sunshine. Bring it into the lives of your men. It is essential and works wonders. It is so easy to do; just a word of encouragement or praise. Catch their interest by making their work agreeable. The secret of training and the object to be aimed at is to make a man like his work. What do you think of the Instructor who is always nagging? Does he get the best out of you? Think of the bullying Instructor? You hate him. Can you put your soul into work you dislike? In time it becomes loathsome.

We have a ready made/national system of training - a British system understood and loved by our men. A system which catches our interest and which develops the highest and noblest qualities for war and life. We must make the most of it. We must organize it, continue to improve it, and never lose sight of the high ideals which govern it. It is the duty of the officer to do all this, it is his sacred trust. He must be the 'live' wire who inspires and leads his men. He will learn to work for his men and lead them, after work as well as during work hours. It will develop his power of leadership. Without the personality to lead, an Officer is useless. Never mind how learned he may be. Leadership can only be developed by practicing leadership, actually leading men in every phase of their life.

What must a leader be able to instil in his men? Trust and comradeship. Take for example a keen young Platoon Commander. He makes up his mind to have the best platoon in the battalion. He takes his men on the square, which unfortunately is often considered the commencement and finish of soldiers. There is the 'dud' late for parade, with dirty buttons; late sloping arms. 'Damn that man, he ruins the platoon, I will knock hell out of him'! The wretched 'dud' comes in for a bad time. The Officer jumps on him, the Sergeant jumps on him. They feel they must 'make' or 'break' him!

Let us look on the 'dud's' side of it. 'Everything I do is wrong, the Officer has got me set, he is a proper --XXXX-- he is'. It is a bad spirit. Will he follow his Officer in battle and play the game behind his back? No and you can't blame him. Yet the platoon Commander is being justified in being strict. But he only sees one side of the 'dud'. He is a bad leader.

After the parade let the platoon Commander join the men in their games. He is astonished to see the 'dud' playing a good game at back, he is not half a bad player and a good sportsman too. He begins to like and respect the 'dud'. The 'dud' sees the Officer playing the Game he loves and playing a good game too. He changes his opinion about the Officer. He is no more a proper --XXX-- but an old sport. Next day, the 'dud' tries harder and wants to please the Officer. The Officer is more human; gives a word or two of encouragement. He brightens the 'dud's' brain with a little sunshine - the 'dud' is stimulated and works better.

An understanding, commenced on the Football Field, grows up between the two. The greatest, truest fellowship in the world is the fellowship of sportsmen. It is the only true democracy in existence. It is team-work and respect in the field and comradeship and respect of it. It is the spirit we want in the Army for it is the conquering spirit in battle. Thus the young officer learns how to create the first principles of leader-ship - trust and comradeship.

What is the next essential quality of a leader? The knowledge of human nature. The human element is power and has its limitations. Every nature is different. Where can he study the character of his men? Why, in a mimic battle. He sees the smart well-behaved man, reliable and hardworking in barracks, lacking in the sterner qualities required by a soldier in the battle. He sees the untidy man of the platoon, a 'sticker' at the game, just the man for a runner. Hullo, who's that earnest fellow with the pluck of a devil? The old 'dud'. The type that will play the game behind your back in a tight corner and so on, the character of every man is radiated to the platoon Commander. He feels he really begins to know his men, the veneer of the parade is dropped, and the material of his platoon is exposed to him. The men sum of their leader - a consensus of 50 opinions. He is summed up as a good sportsman, and pluck to the backbone. Mutual understanding is established.

Another essential quality in a leader is to be able to organize. What is organization? It is imagination, plus a grasp of details. It can be developed by training the brain, by practicing how to organize, organizing platoon games, Boxing and Athletic Meetings, tournaments, keeping records, issuing notices, etc, all of which develop the imagination and increase the grasp of detail.

A leader must have force of character and personality. This can only be developed by constant exercise of will power and personality over the men. Not by driving the men, but by first getting their sympathy, then catching their interest and flaming it into enthusiasm. Nothing is so catching as enthusiasm. The spirit of one man will kindle a flame of enthusiasm throughout an Army. It is the soul of leadership. Men will work on parade during the hours of work, but can you get the men to work for you out of work hours? If you can, you have the making of a leader. You must do this by force of example. I know it is a hard job. You have done a good morning's work. You want to go off to Golf, to tennis or some other amusement. Why should you give up this and get games up for the men? Can't they do it for themselves? It is good for them to see so much of their Officers? These are rotten excuses and not worthy of a leader of men. No, a leader means one who shows the way. If you want your men to give up their time and play the game, you must give them the lead. If you cannot practice self-denial you will not be able to convince your men to do it. Don't be disheartened if they don't respond all at once. They won't. It is your will- the will of a leader - which must conquer them. Stick it, and turn up at the Boxing Club if only one man turns up. Keep on turning up, they will respond in time. Once your spirit of enthusiasm gets into your men, it will spread and you will have won a great fight.

7. Platoon organization for sport.

I offer some suggestions which may be helpful in running the sports in a platoon. First and foremost all sports must be voluntary. Remember games are the life blood of a Briton. It should not be a difficult matter to get every man to play. The spirit of sport is the voluntary spirit. Don't use Bosche methods, for you will stifle that spirit. Endeavour to make everything in connection with sport voluntary. It is the voluntary spirit, the spirit of the 'one more effort' which has made us what we are. Cherish it. Don't centralize the whole work of running the game on your-self you know the ideals of sport; you must be the inspiring spirit of sport and the guiding influence. Trust the men and get them to help you in running their own games. Form your own Platoon Sports Board with you as President. Select Captains and Sub-Captains for all the sports that you are going to include in the Sports Programme, and make them members of the Board. Get as many men as possible 'pushing in the scrum'!! Insist that all sport is carried out in voluntary hours, never let them off parade to train or practice for their games. This is a contemptible form of bribery and the antithesis of true sport. Set the example yourself by working for sport in your leisure hours. You can't be a leader unless you put in an extra hour or two. The men will follow suit. You will create a splendid spirit.

8. The public school spirit.

Inculcate the Public School Spirit into all the Games. Teach the men to 'play the game' to help the Referee and not to work against him. To be chivalrous to a beaten opponent; to be modest when they win. They will soon 'tumble' to it and you will find they are even quixotic. If you cannot run games on these lines you'd better not have them.

9. Specializing in players.

Next don't specialize in any form. Your object is to get as many men as possible to take part in games. To raise the 'dud' to an average standard, instead of neglecting and concentrating on the experts. Get the experts to help you in raising the standard of the whole platoon, give them an opportunity and rely on them, and you will find they will help you. Get as many men as possible to enter into the boxing; have unlimited entries for the cross-country running; organize all games and sports so that they are decided by the side which is most sporting and enters most average competitors and not by the side that relies on a few specialists.

10. Specializing in games.

Don't specialize in only running a few games. Include as many games as practical in the Sports Programme for the year and give every type of man a chance. A man may not be of the right build for football, but can be trained into a good runner. Boxing may not appeal to another who may be useful at Tug-of-war or basket-ball and so on. At least seven or eight different kinds or games and competitions should be included. The following games are all practical in any Garrison at Home or Abroad; Football, Hockey, Athletics, Cross-country, running, basket-ball, wrestling, etc,.

11. Money prizes.

A baneful influence on sport is money prizes. It is another form of bribery. There are some people who advocate money prizes, with the excuse that men won't take an interest in sport unless they get money prizes!! An insult to the man, to sport, and to our intelligence! It is the worst form of specializing and the seed of commercialism in sport - the incubus of sport.

There are several types who advocate Money Prizes. First, the ignorant type with no knowledge of sport. He generally ruins games because he may be well meaning and have a certain amount of spare energy ulterior motive of his own. We have often 'bumped' this type. 'You must give men money prizes' he says, 'But why? Officers will compete for Cups and Medals for the love of the game and honour of their side, why can't men? 'Because they are different' you tell him there are just as big a proportion of sportsmen among the men as among the Officers, if they are only given the education and opportunity. If he is an honest man, he admits this, with regard to all sport, but Boxing. With regard to the latter he may say 'But you can't expect men to knock each other about unless you give them money prizes'. When he says this 'He shows his hand' He wants educating more than the men! He should see the public school boxing, the Army Championships. He will see men get knocked about, but not for anything, but for something far more precious than money prizes - the honour of their side. A man will fight far harder and with far greater spirit for his platoon - fifty men - than he will for himself - one man!!

Remember there is a type of man - I am one of them who like boxing, and instead of having to be paid to be 'knocked out' actually pays another to knock him about!! We like it!

We come to another type who advocates the money prizes. The lazy individual. He realises it is far easier to put some money in an envelope and hand it to the winner of a competition than to select or design appropriate cups or medals, or to educate his men to the ideals of sport and kindle their enthusiasm. The third type is the most dangerous type of all. The individual whose commercial instincts smother his instincts of sport. I don't mean the man who actually completes for a purse or money prize, but the type who has never played a game. He realises there is 'money in it'. He organizes boxing shows, football matches or any form of sport which will draw the public, not for the benefit of sport as he advertises, but for his own benefit. He may get hold of and be 'manager' or parasite, to some prominent boxer or athlete. While the victim is a 'paying proposition' the parasite will cling to him and 'suck' all his earnings and then leave him in the lurch when he has been sucked dry. The victims include boxers, under contract to some promoter, footballers signed on by some commercial syndicate, runners, wrestlers, simmers, rowers, etc, managed by some enterprising financier. The best performers, instead of being educated and trained into professors of sport, have their ideals smothered and are lost to sport.

We see this on every hand outside the Army. If we are not careful the influence of commercialism will affect the Army. We must fight it tooth and nail. Remember the essence of defence is offensive. Why should not the wholesome influence of commercialism in Sport in this Country. The two influences cannot work together. We must 'out' commercialism. We have our ideals, let us put them in practice and commence with the Platoon.

Notes

1 Fighting Fit! Physical Training in the British Army, 1860–1914

1. J. D. Campbell, *The Army Isn't All Work: Physical Culture and the Evolution of the British Army, 1860–1920* (Farnham: Ashgate, 2012) pp. 10–11.
2. Major-General R. S. S. Baden-Powell, *Sport in War* (London: Heinemann, 1900).
3. J. D. Campbell, pp. 19–20.
4. J. D. Campbell, p. 24.
5. A. R. Skelly, *The Victorian Army at Home: The Recruitment and Terms and Conditions of the British Regular, 1859–1899* (London: Croom Helm, 1977) p. 58.
6. W. M. Spiers, *The Late Victorian Army, 1868–1902* (Manchester: Manchester University Press, 1992) p. 131.
7. W. M. Spiers, p. 145.
8. A. R. Skelly, p. 54.
9. J. D. Campbell, pp. 30–31.
10. Report on Gymnastic Instruction in the French and Prussian Armies, August 1859.
11. See E. A. L. Oldfield, *History of the Army Physical Training Corps* (Aldershot: Gale & Polden, 1955).

2 The 'Yellow Peril': Manual of Physical Training, 1908 & NCO's Table Card, 1908

1. E. A. L. Oldfield, *History of the Army Physical Training Corps* (Aldershot: Gale & Polden, 1955) p. 18.
2. Captain B. Williams, *Physical & Bayonet Training*, 1917 (Royal Army Physical Training Corps Museum. Acc. No. 1664) p. 4.

3 Special & Supplementary Tables for Physical Training, 1914–17
1. E. A. L. Oldfield, *History of the Army Physical Training Corps* (Aldershot: Gale & Polden, 1955) p. 22.
2. Captain B. Williams, *Physical & Bayonet Training*, 1917 (Royal Army Physical Training Corps Museum. Acc. No. 1664) p. 7.
3. Colonel W. Wright, *Letter to Captain B. Williams, War Office, 1917* (Royal Army Physical Training Corps Museum. Acc. No. 1664). Regarding alterations to the history of the Physical & Bayonet Staff for official use by the War Office.

4 Bayonet Training, 1916–18
1. E. A. L. Oldfield, *History of the Army Physical Training Corps* (Aldershot: Gale & Polden, 1955) p. 25.
2. Captain B. Williams, *Physical & Bayonet Training*, 1917 (Royal Army Physical Training Corps Museum. Acc. No. 1664) p. 6.
3. Captain F. Starr, *Appendix 'A', The Physical & Recreational Training Staff in France, 1919* (Royal Army Physical Training Corps Museum. Acc. No. 1664) p. 6.
4. E. A. L. Oldfield, p. 42.

5 The 'Spirit of the Bayonet'
1. J. G. Gray, *Prophet in Plimsoles: An Account of the Life of Colonel Ronald B. Campbell* (Edinburgh, Edina Press, 1978) p. 25.
2. S. Sassoon, *Memoirs of an Infantry Officer* (1930) p. 6.
3. J. G. Gray, p. 28.

6 Methods of Unarmed Attack and Defence, 1917
1. See, J. G. Gray, *Prophet in Plimsoles: An Account of the Life of Colonel Ronald B. Campbell* (Edinburgh, Edina Press, 1978).
2. See, G. de Relwyskow, *The Art of Wrestling* (Aldershot: Gale & Polden, 1925).

7 Recreational Training & Games
1. Captain F. Starr, *Appendix 'A', The Physical & Recreational Training Staff in France, 1919* (Royal Army Physical Training Corps Museum. Acc. No. 1664) p. 8.
2. T. Mason & E. Riedi, *Sport and the Military: The British*

Armed Forces 1880-1950 (Cambridge: Cambridge University Press, 2010) p. 18.

3. The Recreational Training S.S. pamphlet 137 was produced in 1918 and would form the final chapter in the 1918 *Physical Training* pamphlet reprinted in October 1918. It is the later of these pamphlets which has been reproduced.

4. Captain F. Starr, p. 9.

5. E. A. L. Oldfield, *History of the Army Physical Training Corps* (Aldershot: Gale & Polden, 1955) p. 35.

9 The Value of Games in Training for War

1. T. Mason & E. Riedi, *Sport and the Military: The British Armed Forces 1880-1950* (Cambridge: Cambridge University Press, 2010) p. 80.

Bibliography

Baden-Powell, Major-General R. S. S., *Sport in War* (London: Heinemann, 1900).

Campbell, J. D., *The Army Isn't All Work: Physical Culture and the Evolution of the British Army, 1860–1920* (Farnham: Ashgate, 2012).

De Relwyskow, G., *The Art of Wrestling* (Aldershot: Gale & Polden, 1925).

Gray, J. G., *Prophet in Plimsoles: An Account of the Life of Colonel Ronald B. Campbell* (Edinburgh, Edina Press, 1978).

Mason, T. & Riedi, E., *Sport and the Military: The British Armed Forces 1880–1950* (Cambridge: Cambridge University Press, 2010).

Oldfield, E. A. L., *History of the Army Physical Training Corps* (Aldershot: Gale & Polden, 1955).

Sassoon, S., *Memoirs of an Infantry Officer* (1930)

Skelly, A. R., *The Victorian Army at Home: The Recruitment and Terms and Conditions of the British Regular, 1859–1899* (London: Croom Helm, 1977).

Spiers, W. M., *The Late Victorian Army, 1868–1902* (Manchester: Manchester University Press, 1992).

Starr, Captain F., *Appendix 'A', The Physical & Recreational Training Staff in France, 1919* (Royal Army Physical Training Corps Museum. Acc. No. 1664).

The National Archives, WO33/14: Report on Gymnastic Instruction in the French and Prussian Armies, August 1859.

Williams, Captain B., *Physical & Bayonet Training, 1917* (Royal Army Physical Training Corps Museum. Acc. No. 1664).

Wright, Colonel W., Letter to Captain B. Williams, War Office, 1917 (Royal Army Physical Training Corps Museum. Acc. No. 1664).

Also available from Amberley Publishing

How to fly the legendary fighter plane in combat using the manuals and instructions supplied by the RAF during the Second World War

'A Must' *INTERCOM: THE AIRCREW ASSOCIATION*

An amazing array of leaflets, books and manuals were issued by the War Office during the Second World War to aid pilots in flying the Supermarine Spitfire, here for the first time they are collated into a single book with the original 1940s setting. An introduction is supplied by expert aviation historian Dilip Sarkar. Other sections include aircraft recognition, how to act as an RAF officer, bailing out etc.

£9.99 Paperback
40 illustrations
264 pages
978-1-84868-436-2

Also available as an ebook
Available from all good bookshops or to order direct
Please call **01453-847-800**
www.amberleybooks.com

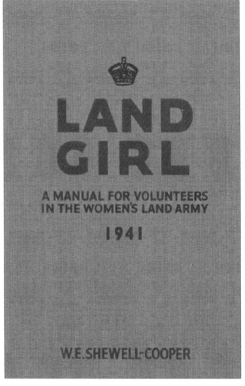